LAKELAND *to* LINDISFARNE

LAKELAND *to* LINDISFARNE
A Coast to Coast Walk from Ravenglass to Holy Island

John Gillham

The Crowood Press

First published in 1995 by
The Crowood Press Ltd
Ramsbury, Marlborough
Wiltshire SN8 2HR

British Library Cataloguing in Publication Data

A catalogue record of this book is available from the British Library.

ISBN 1 85223 871 2

Picture Credits.

Photographs are by the author with the exception of those in Nicola's Diary which have been taken by Nicola Gillham.

Acknowledgments

I would like to thank those who have helped me in the production of this book. Arthur Wood (Ramblers' Association in Berwick, Andrew Miller (Northumberland National Park), Clive Large (Forest Enterprise) and Peter Howe (Northumberland County Council) for help with problem routes through Northumberland. Jeremy Ashcroft for his advice on producing maps on my computer. Last but not least, special thanks must go to my wife, Nicola, who has accompanied me on countless trips in all sorts of weather and found time to write an account of our journey, Lakeland to Lindisfarne.

Front Cover: Looking from the summit of Scafell Pike to the head of Eskdale and Bowfell Pike.
Frontispiece: On Scafell Pike.
Back Cover: Bamburgh Castle in the early morning sun.

Printed and bound by Paramount Printing Group, Hong Kong.
Colour Separation by Next Graphic Limited, Hong Kong.

INTRODUCTION

What could be better on a long-distance walker's itinerary than a coast-to-coast route from the beautiful English Lakes to the wild and rugged Northumbrian coastline; a route that seeks out history and pageant and gives you the opportunity to tackle England's highest mountain? Well, throw in some dramatic coastal castles, some little known verdant dales and a pilgrims'route across the sands, offer both low and mountain routes and you have the 180-mile Lakeland to Lindisfarne route.

There is no doubt that the Lake District has England's most beautiful hills and rightly deserves its popularity. But there is so much beautiful scenery outside the National Park. How many walkers are familiar with Allendale, a leafy glen in the quietest recesses of southern Northumberland, or perhaps Hexhamshire Common?

A long while ago I planned a three-week walk from Ravenglass to Edinburgh – a really tough route across some pretty remote country. I did all the spadework: I bought all the maps, researched the access and accommodation and tried out some of the fiddly bits. I didn't ever get to do the walk that year; I got married instead. Somehow Ravenglass to Edinburgh was forgotten.

After completing books on Snowdonia to Gower and Pennine Ways I looked at the route again. 'It's probably too long,' Nicola said and I agreed. Out came the maps again. 'Maybe we could come off the Cheviots to Wooler and the Northumberland coast?'

I had lived in Newcastle for five years in the seventies and I knew all about the beautiful Northumberland coastline. I had never been to the Simonside ridge though, and its discovery was a revelation. I was captivated by those craggy sandstone peaks cloaked with purple heather – they just had to be included.

I suppose I got greedy for the coast and soon I was omitting the Cheviots in order to see the castles of Alnwick, Dunstanburgh and Bamburgh. Omitting the

Opposite: Lingmell from some pools at Sty Head above Wasdale. Below: The Langdale Pikes from Loughrigg Fell, seen in Chapter 3.

Craster harbour, one of the many fascinating places encountered on the Northumberland coast.

Cheviots! Well I suppose I backed down on that a bit and added a Cheviot Loop alternative for the peak baggers.

I was going to end the route at Bamburgh but, once there, you look out to sea and there it is – a castle on this offshore island. It is Holy Island (formerly Lindisfarne) of course, and it just cannot be left out. So there it was – in perfect alliteration - Lakeland to Lindisfarne.

Having planned the route, Nicola and I tried it out in its entirety. As expected the Lakeland paths worked to perfection, though the weather was less than perfect. After struggling through one of Cross Fell's famous Helm Winds the weather closed in.

We were pleased that most of the planned paths existed underfoot and we strode (or maybe we splashed) though the mists and the rain on a compass bearing.

The Northumberland countryside, away from the National Park and the coast, was littered with blocked and overgrown paths. Rape – the bright yellow stuff looks great from a train or car window but have you ever tried walking through it after a rainstorm or in the early morning dew? You need your waterproof leggings as well as a sense of humour. I had to omit many, many miles of so called 'path' in the countryside between Hexham and Bamburgh but I suppose it made me work that bit harder and I probably ended up with a better line for my troubles.

Ravenglass on the Cumbrian coast is an ideal starting point. It is a quiet little place: most of the noise comes from the seagulls and waves lapping against the

CONTENTS

tackle Scafell Pike itself – an arduous but rewarding challenge for the backpacker. This could also include Esk Pike and the Langdales.

Ambleside may be a bit of a tourist trap but it's an interesting tourist trap, and conveniently placed to restock supplies. The next range to be tackled is High Street via Troutbeck and Kentmere. The lower route straddles Nan Bield Pass and traces the edge of Haweswater; the higher route treads the delectable ridges. High Street is probably the best ridge walk in Lakeland – a must for all Lakeland to Lindisfarners on settled, sunny days.

Crossing the evergreen Eden Valley gives you the chance for respite from the cruel ups and downs. There are some splendid villages, Morland and Temple Sowerby in particular.

But its up those stairs again! Cross Fell at over 2930ft (893m) is the highest Pennine; even on the lower route you have to climb to over 2500ft (750m). It is worth the effort, if only for the views back to the Lakeland peaks you have just left. Miners' tracks take you down vast and stark hillsides to Garrigill. On the direct low route you will meet Pennine Wayers; on the high route by the banks of Trout Beck, you will almost certainly meet no one.

The George and Dragon at Garrigill is one of my favourite pubs – good ambiance, good food, plenty of it and not too expensive. Even if you decide not to stay, do spend an evening here for you're bound to meet some new friends.

Few walkers will have any knowledge of the next section, which traverses the lonely moors into Allendale, a valley not too dissimilar to the dales of Yorkshire. Here you will see a lovely little waterfall, Holm Linn, and a village, Allendale Town, with a fiery tradition.

Hexham is a buzzing historical market town in the heart of the Tyne Valley. It's a grand place, dominated by the abbey and the wide river. Beyond it, low routes weave their way amid the undulating farmlands of the North Tyne and Redesdale. Reminders of a turbulant past – battles with the Scots and the murderous Border Reivers – are never far away.

Simonside, as I have mentioned previously, is more spectacular stuff – a return to the hills. You can see both the coast and the Cheviots from its heather-clad summits.

Which way now? Well, the lower route descends to Rothbury, one of the prettiest villages in Northumberland. The high route, strangely enough,

sand dunes. Unlike that other coast-to-coast, it takes less than an hour to get to the first summit, Muncaster Fell. The splendid little peak is studded with crag, bracken and the odd twisted mountain ash. After descending to Eskdale Green the middle of the day is spent climbing through mixed woodland to the hills above Wastwater. The end of the day is spent on the descent from Illgill Head into Wasdale Head, a mountain arena, guarded by England's highest tops, including Scafell, Scafell Pike and Great Gable. You can spend a memorable night on the seats outside the Wasdale Head Inn with a contemplative pint watching the last of the sun's rays flickering over the serrated mountain crests.

On the next section you can follow the old trade routes by way of Sty Head into Great Langdale or begins low, along the valley of the Coquet to Alwinton. Here it climbs along ancient Clennell Street to the Cheviot ridge at Windy Gyle, thence over the Cheviot itself and into Wooler. It meets the coast at Beal and immediately crosses over to Holy Island.

The lower route continues from Rothbury to Edlingham, a secluded village with its own little castle. Next stop is Alnwick, a majestic place full of history and pageant. Home to the Percy family, its riverside castle is truly magnificent. From Alnwick it is just a half day to the coast at Boulmer then it's easy walking all the way. The coast cannot be hurried, though; there is just too much to see, too many rock pools to examine for crabkind; proud cliffs, quiet bays, small fishing villages and large castles all wait to be discovered round that next cove. You will *have* to taste the famous Craster kippers, said to be the best in the world (by the people of Craster, of course).

Holy Island has a special presence, but stay the night or it may be lost among the throngs of the day trippers who flock here like flotsam with the tide. Its fairy-tale castle, priory ruins and maritime aura make this a fitting end to a walk that has brought us from Ravenglass to Holy Island, from Lakeland to Lindisfarne.

I have divided the route into thirteen chapters plus one chapter for the Cheviot Loop alternative. Although these sections would make a feasible schedule they are largely for the convenience of the book layout. Choose the schedule that is convenient to you.

My maps are not intended for use in the field – there is not enough detail for that. Use them to plot your intended route on the Ordnance Survey maps.

Accommodation available is constantly changing. Rather than list what is available at present I have included the telephone numbers of the relevant tourist information centres in the planning chart in the appendix. The centres will send you up-to-date lists. The route files also show the distance and time required to walk the route covered by the chapter, an overview of the terrain, possible escape routes (in the mountain sections) and the shops available.

The low-level Lakeland to Lindisfarne route is not a difficult one. It is about on a par with Wainwright's Coast to Coast and much easier than the Pennine Way. The mountain route is tougher, especially in the Scafell Pike area, where the ridges are boulder-strewn. In good weather conditions most walkers will want to include some of the peaks – it is just a matter of knowing one's own limitations and keeping track of the weather forecasts. Tailor the route to meet your own requirements; *do* make changes if there is somewhere off-route that you want to visit. This is no hard line across the country. Let's hope that you will be blessed with good weather and will soon be triumphantly following in the footsteps of St Cuthbert and St Aidan across the sands to Lindisfarne.

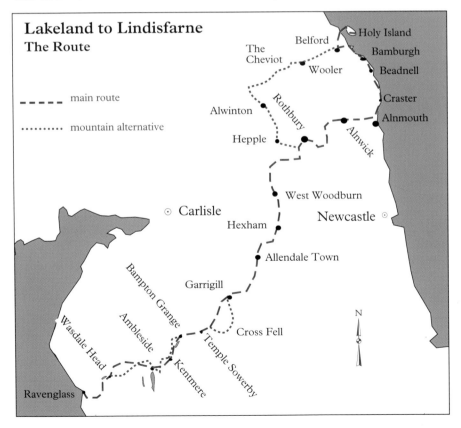

Lakeland to Lindisfarne
The Route

- - - - - main route

.... mountain alternative

1

FROM COAST TO MOUNTAIN COUNTRY

Ravenglass to Wasdale Head

Ravenglass echoes to the sound of the waves, seagulls, and maybe the shoosh of a steam engine getting ready to carry wide-eyed children on a journey through Eskdale. Braced by the salty sea air we are ready for our marathon journey. This will take us into the mountainous regions of Lakeland, the highest Pennines and the ancient kingdom of Northumbria and the Holy Isle of Lindisfarne.

The first section is a gentle one. It begins with an easy stroll through the woodlands of the Muncaster Estate and is followed by a climb to Muncaster Fell, a Lakeland ridge in miniature but with mountain views as grand as they come.

After descending to Eskdale Green the route climbs though the forest and clambers onto the ridges above Wasdale. The gulleys of Whin Rigg give the first teasing glimpses of Wastwater whilst the descent from Illgill Head takes us into the magnificent arena of Wasdale Head, where England's highest mountains impose themselves like temples in the sky.

The Wastwater Screes, which form the savage north-western facade of Whin Rigg and Illgill Head.

RAVENGLASS TO WASDALE HEAD
The Main Route

Situated at the mouth of an estuary into which flow the rivers Irt, Esk and Mite, Ravenglass, once a thriving Roman port, has known busier times. This place is famed for its narrow-gauge railway, the first in England.

A quiet evening stroll down the picturesque Main Street to the seashore is a must to get the tranquil mood of this place. Looking out to sea beyond the small boats and sand dunes you may be lucky enough to witness one of the west coast's celebrated sunsets.

RAVENGLASS
Take the ginnel heading eastwards from Main Street over the railway and behind the narrow-gauge station. Perhaps there is time to see 'Ratty's' quaint little steam engines.

On reaching a junction close to the road (GR 087965), turn right onto the track which leads though a narrow strip of woodland, the Walls Plantation.

NB If the tide is out you will be able to cut a corner by following the shoreline to the left from the southern tip of Main Street to a narrow path, which then strikes eastwards into Walls Plantation. It meets the previously described route at GR 087962 where you turn right.

The path continues southwards past the ruins of the Roman bath house, all that remains of Walls Castle. After taking a left fork, the route approaches the large mansion of Newtown. The track we want now heads north-eastwards through the decorative woodlands of the Muncaster Castle estate then through more open land.

MUNCASTER FELL
Turn left to reach the A595 by Home Farm (GR 096966) then right along the road for a third of a mile (500m) to a sharp bend. Here continue on a track, Fell Lane, which climbs north-eastwards towards Muncaster Fell. As height is gained retrospective views widen. The Cumbrian coastline and the chequered pastures of the plains are dissected by the estuaries and meandering courses of the Rivers Esk and Mite. In the distance the outlines of Sellafield remind us of issues we would prefer to tuck away on days such as this.

Muncaster Tarn and its neighbouring coniferous plantations are left behind and we enter the world of fell and mountain. The path passes to the south of Hooker Crag's top but it's a worthwhile short detour for the

Ravenglass, seen at low tide across the Mite Estuary. The hill on the horizon is Black Combe.

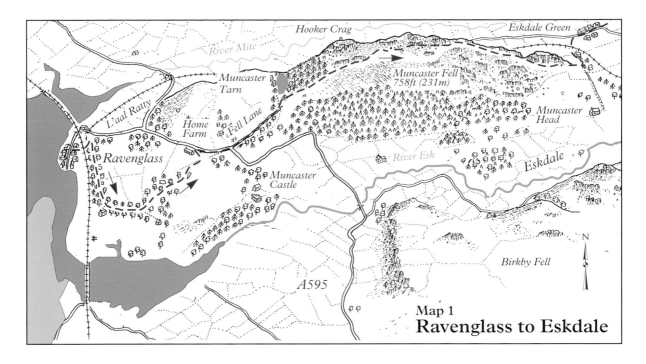

Map 1
Ravenglass to Eskdale

On Muncaster Fell, a true Lakeland ridge, but of miniature proportions. Across Eskdale you can see Harter Fell dominating the horizon.

Eskdale – The Romans, Ratty and Muncaster

The Romans came to Cumbria in the first century AD. Their fort of Glannaventa, sited to the south of modern-day Ravenglass, was one of many guarding the Cumbrian Coast. These served as an extension to the fortresses of Hadrian's Wall, which ended at Bowness-on-Solway. Ravenglass was soon established as their regional naval base. They built a road through the Lakeland Hills linking Glannaventa with Galava (at Waterhead), passing through high Eskdale to the spartan and remote fort of Hardknott. This joined another of their roads, High Street (they knew it as Brettestrete – the Britons' Road), which climbed to well over 2000ft (600m) onto the Far Eastern Fells before descending to Brocavarum (Brougham) near Penrith. Our route through the lakes will often coincide with these Roman highways.

Today all that remains of Glannaventa is the bath house, yet this red sandstone building with 12ft walls is ironically one of the best-preserved Roman buildings in Northern England.

Nearby Muncaster Castle is surrounded by beautiful woods and gardens filled with colourful rhododendrons and azaleas. The pele tower dates back to the fourteenth century and stands on Roman foundations. The castle was extended throughout the following centuries: much of it, including the more modern tower, was built in the mid-nineteenth century by Anthony Salvin, an architect well known for 'modernizing castles'.

The castle has been in the hands of the Pennington family since 1325. Henry VI is said to have sheltered here in 1464 following his defeat at the Battle of Hexham. According to legend he was led down from Muncaster Fell by a humble shepherd and rested for nine days. In gratitude he left his drinking bowl behind. This glass bowl, decorated with gold and enamel, is known as the Luck of Muncaster and it is said that as long as it remains intact the Penningtons will live and thrive in the place.

Ravenglass continued to flourish as a port until the industrial revolution. It was once known for its smugglers. These days it is synonymous with 'L'aal Ratty', the old steam-driven narrow-gauge railway which chugs through Eskdales magnificent scenery all the way to Boot. Constructed in 1875 as a 3ft gauge line to convey iron-ore, it was converted in 1915 to a 15in gauge. The original mine closed and Ratty was used to carry passengers and pink Eskdale granite from the quarries at Beckfoot.

In 1960 there was a threat of closure. The day was saved when the line was bought by a Preservation Society with the help of Colin Gilbert and Lord Wakefield. It has since been successfully operated as a tourist attraction.

One of the steam engines on the Ravenglass and Eskdale Railway seen here on the turntable at Ravenglass. Once a working line L'aal Ratty, as it is affectionately known, is now a tourist attraction.

Eskdale Green seen on the approach from Muncaster Fell.

views and maybe a refreshment stop; if you didn't over-sleep there should be no hurry today.

Looking down Eskdale, the narrowing sliver of green that surrounds the meandering river weaves through the crusty crags and bluffs that rise to the shapely cone of Harter Fell. In the opposite direction the soaring whale back of Illgill Head leads the eye to Scafell and the high western peaks.

The well-defined path continues over rough moor grass and bracken. It passes between crag, outcrop and the odd wind-warped rowan or hawthorn before reaching a track linking Muncaster Head and Hollowstones.

ESKDALE GREEN

Turn left along the track, which descends northwards through bushes of gorse, then past the Foresthow Country House Hotel and Irton Green station on the 'Ratty Line'. Here a lane leads to the road west of Eskdale Green, a pleasant village sheltered by an afforested knoll and accompanied by a small lake. There's accommodation available and they have a post office, general store and outdoor gear shop (you may have found out what you have forgotten to bring by now).

After passing through the village, follow the sign-posted walled track from GR 142002 at the edge of woodland, passing Low Holme Farm before descending to the Miterdale Bridleway. Go straight across the road and follow the footpath northwards across the single-arched stone bridge over the River Mite. From here the clear path veers to the left before climbing through broad-leafed woodland. Several flinted forestry tracks are crossed on a steep ascent towards Irton Fell. The upper part of the plantations consist mainly of conifers, but there is the odd clearing with scattered crags to maintain the interest.

On reaching open fell, the little village of Nether Wasdale comes into view in the valley below. For those seeking nearby accommodation, there are two inns, a country house hotel (Lowood Hall) and a youth hostel (GR145045)on the shores of Wastwater. Unless time is short, I would recommend a stop at Wasdale Head

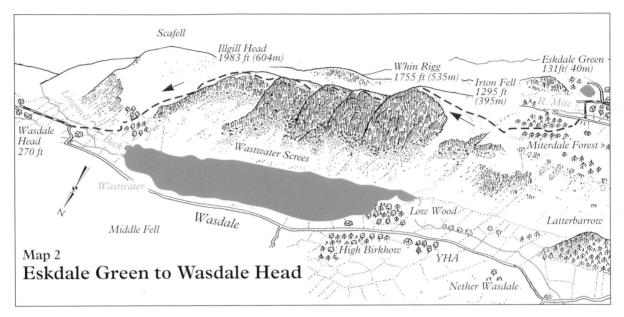

Map 2
Eskdale Green to Wasdale Head

however. Besides being scenically superior it shortens tomorrow's more demanding schedule. If you intend to tackle the mountain route over Scafell Pike and the Langdales this is especially important.

WHIN RIGG
A prominent track twenty yards or so north of the forest gate climbs the rough, grassy slopes of Irton Fell. Beyond the rocky cleft of Great Hall Gill the ascent of the more shapely Whin Rigg begins and we get glimpses of Wastwater far below. The summit is gained fairly easily on good paths over firm, grassy terrain. The summit cairn is set precariously close to the edge of precipitous cliffs, which plummet 1500ft (450m) into the deep, dark waters of Wastwater. The lake is enveloped by verdant plains at the foot of Lakeland's finest and most shapely fells – Yewbarrow, Kirk Fell, Pillar, Great Gable, Lingmell and Scafell.

ILLGILL HEAD
The continuation of the ridge route towards Illgill Head is highlighted by more spectacular gullies, plunging to the depths of the lake. After descending to a depression at just over 1500ft (450m) (adorned by two small tarns), more good paths climb to the pile of stones that crowns the lush, grassy summit of Illgill Head. Views of Wasdale Head are more intimate and rewarding than ever. The whitewashed inn is dwarfed by the unrelent-

ing ramparts of Kirk Fell. Great Gable brings up the rear, proudly wearing its bold crags like a king wears his crown. From this viewpoint Gable is in every sense a monarch, for Scafell furtively hides its gigantic buttresses behind gentle grassy flanks. To the east the remote lake of Burnmoor Tarn lies in a marshy bowl beneath the crags of Eskdale Fell and at the head of Miterdale. This is said to be the mountain country described in *Swallows and Amazons*.

The descent on the grassy north-eastern flanks of Illgill Head is steep but easy. The bridleway from Miterdale is met on the pass to the north of Burnmoor Tarn and the route heads northwards, descending to the perimeters of Fence Wood.

WASDALE
A stony path now leads down into the valley, passing some ruins *en route* to Brackenclose, which is kept to the right. Wastwater is seen to the west but from this low viewpoint it has lost its magic. You *will* be spellbound by views to the east. Here the mighty cliffs, gullies and screes of both Scafell (left) and Scafell Pike (right) fill the skyline at the head of a barren ravine cut by Lingmell Gill. The steely scene is often tempered by yellow splashes of gorse and the verdant foliage of trees that surround the plains of Wasdale.

Lingmell Gill is crossed via a footbridge at GR183074. Take the path to the right, which follows

Looking down the ravine between Broad Crag and the summit of Whin Rigg to the south-western tip of Wastwater and Wasdale Hall.

the edge of the campsite, before crossing Lingmell Beck (usually dry). It continues through scrubland and gorse to meet the narrow lane a quarter of a mile (400m) short of Wasdale Head. The large whitewashed inn is surrounded by a cluster of stone cottages and an outdoor shop and is usually buzzing with walkers and mountaineers.

WASDALE HEAD

The inn was once owned by Will Ritson, a colourful character with a penchant for tall stories. Today Wasdale continues his tradition by holding the 'Biggest Liar in the World' competition. Fell runner Jos Naylor, who lives on a farm at the foot of Yewbarrow, once won it with his story about crossing Herdwick sheep with kangaroos to produce herdaroos.

The little church of St Olaf, lying at the valley head and sheltered by yew trees, is said to have roof beams that were salvaged from the wreckage of Viking ships. The churchyard has many climbers' graves – some died in tragic mountaineering accidents. There are also memorials to Himalayan climbers. One of the windows has an etching of Napes Needle on Great Gable with the words, 'I will lift up mine eyes unto the hills from whence cometh my strength.'

The village as a whole is probably in the most spectacular setting in all England with many of the country's highest mountains rearing up from the green fields at

the head of the lake. Hopefully you will have had a good day and will be in fine fettle – eager to tackle tomorrow's most sensational route.

POSSIBLE ALTERNATIVES

If the weather is inclement it is feasible to divert from the main route beyond Low Holme at GR 143008. Here a bridleway heads up Miterdale to climb the moors to the west of Burnmoor Tarn. The main route is met at the pass above the tarn and it is a simple descent into Wasdale. This is a good route with plenty of interest but without those spectacular views down the gullies into Wastwater. The route would be of no use for those looking for youth hostel accommodation at Wasdale Hall.

Those looking for accommodation at the youth hostel and the village of Nether Wasdale will have to descend Irton Fell on the clear bridleway NNW to reach the road at Forest Bridge. The best way to get to Wasdale Head the next day would be to take the path at the foot of the screes along the southern shores of the lake (take care as the screes are loose and the lake is deep and cold!).

Anybody looking for an adventurous and more energetic end to the first day could descend to Wastwater on the path from the col between Irton Pike

The pack-horse bridge at Wasdale Head. Pillar (left) and Kirkfell (right) wear their green summer cloaks.

and Whin Rigg, then follow the bridleway to the high Western Fells along Greendale Gill. They could then climb to Haycock via Middle Fell and Seatallan. It would then be a spectacular route over Pillar to the Black Sail youth hostel. Next day the mountain route could then continue over Great Gable before descending to meet the main route at Angle Tarn. This would mean omitting Scafell Pike (unless the Corridor Route was taken) but it would be feasible to add Allen Crags before the high route over the Langdale Pikes. The distance betweenRavenglass and Black Sail would be 18 miles (30km).

ROUTE FILE

Distance	14 miles (22km)
Time	8 hours
Terrain	Moderate climbs over firm terrain, much of it grassy. Care must be exercised at the cliff edges at Whin Rigg and Illgill Head.
Accommodation	Inn and B&Bs at Eskdale Green and Wasdale Head; 2 official campsites at Wasdale head. Off route - Inns and Youth Hostel at Nether Wasdale
Shops	P.O. & general store at Eskdale Green; outdoor equipment Shops at Eskdale and Wasdale Head

2

ACROSS THE FELLS OF CENTRAL LAKELAND

Wasdale Head to Great Langdale

Yesterday we walked on attractive hills, through villages hewn from Lakeland slate and on pretty woodland paths. Today everything is on a grander scale as we travel through the highest mountains of England.

From Wasdale's great amphitheatre the main route climbs on ancient tracks used by travellers of yesteryear. Great Gable towers to the left of the path, Scafell Pike to the right. You will see the great gash of Piers Gill and the wild corries of Sty Head and Sprinkling Tarn before descending amid sullen crag and tumbling gills to the green fields of Mickleden and Great Langdale.

In settled weather it is feasible for experienced fell-walkers to tackle the mountain tops. The high route climbs Scafell Pike and along the bouldery ridge to Esk Pike. From here you can drop into Langdale or head for the Langdale Pikes via Angle Tarn and Stake Pass. The Blea Rigg ridge which follows is ideal for wild camping. Strong walkers could head for the youth hostel at High Close or one of the B&Bs at Elterwater.

Climbing from Sty Head Pass towards Sprinkling Tarn on the main route with Great Gable filling the horizon.

WASDALE HEAD TO ELTERWATER
The Main Route

WASDALE HEAD

Our way out of Wasdale is spectacular. Right from the start we plot a course amid mountains of grandeur and great presence. The route begins along the eastern banks of Mosedale Beck behind the Wasdale Head Inn, passing the old stone pack-horse bridge and the cottages of Row Head. The beck meanders to the left beneath Kirk Fell, whose steep grassy flanks are only broken by high screes and the furrow of an extremely bold path striking for the skyline. Thankfully, you may say, *our* route follows a shallow, subsidiary stream to the right and we take a last look down spectacular Mosedale to the crusty fellsides of Pillar and Red Pike.

The view ahead is equally inspiring, dominated by the jagged crest that tops Great Gable. The path flirts with both banks of the stream, crossing it on numerous occasions by the way of log bridges. Passing behind Burnthwaite Farm, the valley sides close in and we climb on the lower slopes of Gable. To our right, Lingmell, which looked an uninteresting grassy mound from Wasdale, displays an altogether more appealing, craggy face. The face is rent by a tremendous sickle-shaped ravine – that of Piers Gill. Beyond Lingmell rise the brooding crags and cliffs of England's highest mountain, Scafell Pike.

STY HEAD

We reach Sty Head, a high pass and meeting point of old traders' routes between Wasdale, Borrowdale and Langdale. The scenes are transformed yet again. Below is Sty Head Tarn, a wild sheet of water set uneasily in a grassy bowl and sandwiched by the bluffs and outcrops of Seathwaite Fell and also by the steep, stony slopes of Green Gable. The nick of Borrowdale gives us insights into northern Lakeland but our route veers to the east, parallel with the southern shores of the tarn.

The well-defined path now climbs to Sprinkling Tarn, spectacularly set beneath the gigantic dark cliffs

Leaving Wasdale Head behind on the climb to Sty Head.

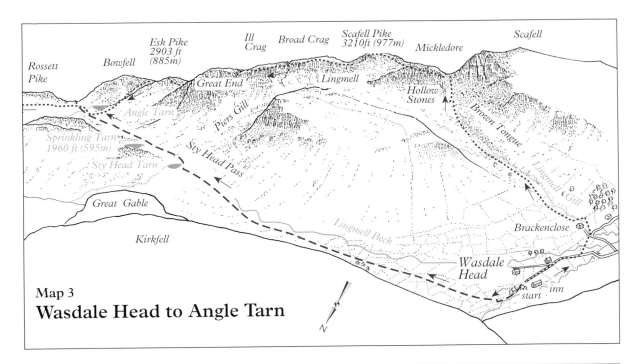

Map 3
Wasdale Head to Angle Tarn

Pack-horse Routes around Wasdale

Wasdale Head is now a quiet backwater of the Lakes, largely the domain of the sheep-farmer and climber. It was not always so for it was once well served by a network of pack-horse routes which threaded through the high fells.

Traders would herd trains of up to twenty ponies on these ancient thoroughfares. The robust ponies, often Galloways, carried panniers filled with slate from Honister, graphite from Borrowdale and local wool bound for the coastal ports. They might return with imports of tobacco and spirits for Ambleside. Some would be legal: some would not, for smuggling was rife in notorious Ravenglass.

The building of the turnpike roads, which were the basis of our modern network, saw the demise of the pack-horse trails. They are now left to the walker, the rider and that new-age traveller, the mountain biker.

A fine example of a pack-horse bridge is still to be found behind the inn at Wasdale Head (*see* photo page 18).

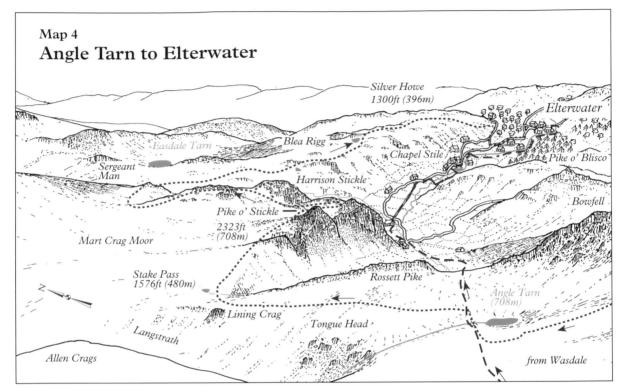

Map 4
Angle Tarn to Elterwater

of Great End, Scafell Pike's abrupt northern ramparts and the rocky bluffs of Seathwaite Fell.

Continuing among the high Lakeland mountains, the path climbs further eastwards past the head of the Grains Gill's cavernous hollow. It then traces the southern edge of a ravine cut by the stream (hereabouts known as Ruddy Gill) to attain the highest point of the day, beneath the rocky slopes of Allen Crags. There is a wind-break shelter here for those in need of a lunch stop.

ANGLE TARN
The wide stony path ahead now descends in the shadow of Esk Pike (R) to Angle Tarn. This superb gem of a tarn lies secretively in a deep basin beneath the sultry, broken cliffs of Hanging Knotts and at the head of another deep hollow, Langstrath, which also offers an escape into Borrowdale. I had thought of advocating an approach to Langdale via Stake Pass from Angle Tarn but decided that it was too circuitous compared with the descent on the Pony path south of Rosset Gill.

From the tarn the path climbs to the col between Rossett Pike and Hanging Knotts then descends towards Mickleden, a long verdant swathe of land flanked by the Langdale Pikes and Bowfell's Band. In the interests of conservation it is better not to follow the masses down the bouldered chute of Rossett Gill but to divert to a well made stony path to the right, which twists and turns amid bluff and grassy shelves beneath Bowfell to join the 'Gill Path' further downhill.

MICKLEDEN
The path from Stake Pass is met at a footbridge. From here the route assumes a level, easy-paced course down Mickleden with Pike o' Stickle's precipitous, crag-crowned scree slopes dominating to the left. Neolithic axe factories existed here. The stone axes, made from the volcanic rock of the fell, were transported to the coast, where they were polished with sandstone before being exported.

THE GREAT LANGDALE VALLEY
As we turn the corner into Great Langdale the valley floor widens and the pastures become more verdant, enclosed by dry-stone walls so typical of Lakeland landscapes. It is difficult not to keep looking back towards

Above: Great Gable and Sty Head Pass in the evening light. Below: Descending into Mickleden near the foot of Rossett Gill.

Great Langdale seen from Spedding Crag with the heather-capped Lingmoor backed up on the horizon by the Coniston Fells .

the serrated mountain tops of Pike o' Blisco, Crinkle Crags and Bow Fell.

As the spur known as the Band declines to Stool End Farm, another side valley, that of Oxendale, comes into view to the right beneath Crinkle Crags and Pike o' Blisco.

Middle Fell Farm is passed and, if we have tremendous will power, so is the Old Dungeon Gill Hotel. (I

have yet to succeed in ignoring this lively hotel during opening hours.)

The enclosed track now continues above the hotel beneath Raven Crag and down to the New Dungeon Gill Hotel (no, this is not a pub crawl!). On the opposite side of the B road beyond the hotel and by a car park, a walled gravel track leads eastwards close to Great Langdale Beck. The track briefly rejoins the

Wainwright Hotel. After following it eastwards for a hundred yards or so, the road is again abandoned to cross the stream via another bridge before continuing through the site of an old slate quarry, now landscaped. The track becomes a tarmac lane and meets a back road from Little Langdale close to Elterwater Youth Hostel.

ELTERWATER

This most pleasant of Langdale villages lies just across the river. There are a few bed and breakfast establishments and a splendid whitewashed inn, the Britannia.

WASDALE HEAD TO ELTERWATER
A Mountain Alternative via Scafell Pike

The climbing of Scafell Pike will be irresistible for many walkers; after all it is England's highest mountain and Wasdale is undoubtably the finest approach. It can be combined with Esk Pike Harrison Stickle and the Blea Rigg ridge for one of the Lake District's classic routes.

It is worth noting at this point that this is the most arduous itinerary of the whole route and should only be undertaken by or in the presence of experienced mountain walkers.

WASDALE HEAD

Retrace yesterday's steps to the the bridge over Lingmell Gill (GR 183074). After crossing it, a short concessionary footpath follows the banks of the stream to meet a right of way from the Wastwater Screes. The path recrosses the stream via a wooden footbridge and continues on a steady climb along the northern banks.

BROWN TONGUE

The chances are that, unless you've made a late start, you will be in shade, but this does nothing to detract from the sullen but spectacular rock scenery ahead. Lower slopes are adorned with broad-leafed trees and bracken but above them are stony hillslopes crowned with the sombre crags of Scafell (R) and its higher offspring, Scafell Pike (L).

The path has had much attention of late and is largely constructed of carefully laid stones, which can be a little slippery in wet or frozen conditions. The stream is crossed once more and the route continues over Brown Tongue, ever deeper into the shady corrie of Hollowstones. As height is gained the vertical cliffs of

road. A short way eastwards along the road we turn right onto a path that heads southwards to cross the beck via a footbridge. It continues across fields close to the riverbanks, passing a campsite before recrossing the river at another bridge close to the slate village of Chapel Stile.

A wide track now heads northwards then veers to the right parallel to the road, which is met by the

Scafell's northern face become more and more imposing and you can look up the narrow cleft of Lord's Rake, which gives access to its summit – another day perhaps?

The last section from Hollowstones to Mickledore, the col between Scafell and the Pike, is steep and the terrain consists of loose red screes. The difficulties are short-lived, however, and soon you are basking in new views across Upper Eskdale to the distinctive peaks of Bowfell and Crinkle Crags.

SCAFELL PIKE

A cairned path over bouldered slopes to the left leads to the summit, which is crowned with a gigantic cairn, many stone shelters and probably a score or more other walkers – this is a popular place. As would be expected from the highest place in England the views are magnificent, especially from the edges. Possibly the finest is that to the north and west, where the domed massif of Great Gable rules supreme in a vista also graced by Pillar and the Mosedale Fells. If it is clear you will be able to pick out the pale profile of the Solway Firth. The piked ridges of Helvellyn and Fairfield cut a dash in views to the right whilst the Coniston Fells lead the eye out to sea over Morecambe Bay and maybe as far as the Isle of Man. If discernible it will be just above and to the right of Scafell Crag. It is time to move on

On the summit of Scafell Pike.

and we continue down boulder-strewn slopes to Broad Crag Col then scramble up to Broad Crag, a subsidiary three-thousand footer. A descent to Ill Crag Col follows before climbing to a gravelly plateau north of Ill Crag.

ESK HAUSE

A short way further the path divides. We want the one to the right (the one to the left continues to Great End), and this descends to the grassy pass, Esk Hause. If you want to transfer to the main Lakeland to Lindisfarne route at the pass, follow the path descending north-eastwards past a cross shelter. Do not confuse this with the preceding cairned route, which heads north-westwards to Sprinkling Tarn.

Those with an appetite for more high fells will continue south-eastwards on a straightforward path to the bouldered top of Esk Pike, where views back to Scafell and Scafell Pike are magnificent. A descent is now made to Ore gap, the pass beneath Bowfell. Many may be tempted with Bowfell but, unless an early descent into Great Langdale is required it is better to head for a longer itinerary over the Langdale Pikes.

ANGLE TARN

The Langdale Pikes route begins with a short northerly descent on a path that meets the main route north-west of Angle Tarn. The path is followed round the northern edge of the tarn before being abandoned for a path to the left, which heads north-eastwards on high, grassy slopes above the deep valley of Langstrath. To the right are the squat peaks of Rosset Pike and Black Crags.

THE STAKE PASS

The well-defined path gradually encircles Langdale Combe before dipping to the small pool at Stake Pass (escape route to the valley).

We're now approaching the Langdale Pikes. First

Lingmell (near left), Kirkfell and cloud-capped Great Gable seen from Broad Crag.
Gimmer Crag seen from Pike o' Stickle with the fields of Great Langdale leading the eye to Lake Windermere near the horizon.

Above: Easdale Tarn from Blea Rigg. Below: Walkers on the Blea Rigg ridge with Harrison Stickle and Pavey Ark on the skyline.

on the list is Pike o' Stickle, Langdale's very own Sugar Loaf Mountain. This shapely dome of crag and buttress rises boldly from the surrounding rough grassland and wild moor.

PIKE O' STICKLE

A good path heads southwards then south-eastwards across Martcrag Moor before clambering the crags of Pike o' Stickle. It's a fine vantage point with spectacular

views over the pastures of Mickleden and the great climbing grounds of Gimmer Crag.

After descending Pike o' Stickle by the ascent route, the path continues along the edge towards Loft Crag (ignore the eroded direct route eastwards to Harrison Stickle). Pike o' Stickle looks just as impressive in retrospect and now has the backdrop of Bowfell and Crinkle Crags for good measure.

HARRISON STICKLE OR THUNACAR KNOTT

On meeting an ascent route from Langdale beneath Loft Crag, turn left (north) on a path that fords the infant Dungeon Gill (usually a mere trickle hereabouts)and continue northwards beneath Harrison Stickle, highest of the Pikes.

Whether or not you include Harrison Stickle depends on your conscience. It's an interesting peak with good views along Great Langdale to Windermere and Morecambe Bay but you will probably have to share them with a multitude of walkers. Nearly all the routes are badly eroded however and could do with a rest. If you must do it, climb the wide stony shoot to the right which will take you to the summit. After scrambling down the rocky northern slopes a well-used route continues NNE to Thunacar Knott. Those who decide not to climb to Harrison Stickle simply continue straight on for Thunacar Knott.

SERGEANT MAN

From here our route heads towards the massive fellsides of High Raise before encircling the wide combe between Pavey Ark and Blea Rigg to the prominent rocky knoll of Sergeant Man. This gives new views over Easdale to Grasmere and the Helvellyn and Fairfield ridges.

BLEA RIGG

The path from Sergeant Man along Blea Rigg is in places very well defined. Occasionally, however, it dives into obscurity, only to reappear a short while later. This presents no difficulty in clear conditions but could be very tricky in mist as the frequent crags and bluffs are hard to differentiate.

From Blea Rigg there are intimate views of both Codale and Easdale Tarns but the attention is generally drawn to the improving views of Stickle Tarn, which lies beneath the craggy 'castles' of Pavey Ark and Harrison Stickle. Our devious route climbs up, down and in between rocky bluffs on the wide ridge between Easdale and Great Langdale. Several remote, windswept pools are passed. Beyond Swinescar Pike and to the south of Lang How we pass the largest of these – a reedy expanse of water with a classic view back to the Langdale Pikes.

The path continues its undulating course, over slightly less craggy terrain now with the summit of Silver Howe directly ahead. On a grassy shelf just beneath this summit, turn right (south) to pick up another track at a huge cairn. This descends to Spedding Crag (unnamed on 1:50000 maps) and Dow Bank. The villages of Elterwater and Chapel Stile can be seen below right amid green pasture and bracken-clad common land.

ELTERWATER

The path continues to meet the road at Red Bank close to the youth hostel – turn left along the road for the hostel and right if you are staying in the village.

POSSIBLE ALTERNATIVES

Mountain Route: From Esk Pike continue along the ridge to Bowfell, then southwards along Crinkle Crags and Cold Pike to the Wrynose Pass. Climb to Swirl Howe and Wetherlam (Coniston Fells) then descend Birk Fell into Little Langdale. A series of paths links Little Langdale with Elterwater. This would be a very long route with much ascent and descent. It would necessitate a wild camp or bivvy on the fells but would be spectacular in the right conditions. Distance from Wasdale head to Elterwater would be 17 miles (26km) and would take at least 12 hours.

ROUTE FILE
Main Route

Distance	12 miles (19 km)
Time	7 hours
Terrain	Although there are no specific difficulties this route climbs to mountainous terrain far from civilization. In mists good navigational skills will be required
Escape Routes	1 From Sty Head into Seathwaite, Borrowdale. 2 From pass south of Sprinkling Tarn to Seathwaite via Grains Gill
Accommodation	Inns: Old Dungeon Gill and New Dungeon Gill (Gt. Langdale); Campsite by Old Dungeon Gill. Campsite, Inn and B&Bs at Chapel Stile; Britannia Inn and B&B at Elterwater; Numerous wild campsites including Sty Head, Sprinkling Tarn and Angle Tarn
Shops	P.O. at Chapel Stile; general store at Elterwater

Mountain Route

Distance	15 miles (24km)
Time	10 hours
Terrain	This is the toughest itinerary of the whole walk and spends much of the day between 2500 and 3200 ft. It includes steep ascents on rocky and bouldery terrain and should only be attempted by the fit and experienced mountain walker
Escape Routes	From Esk Hause down to Seathwaite via Grains Gill
Accommodation	As main route
Shops	As main route

3

THROUGH THE LAKELAND OF THE POETS

Great Langdale to Kentmere

We are now in the heart of the Lakeland that has inspired artists, poets and writers alike; the domain of William Wordsworth and Beatrix Potter – a place of daffodils, woodland and rippling becks; of blue lakes and green-hued slate.

Today our route explores some low, bracken-clad fells punctuated by crusty crags, twisted hawthorns and mountain ash; spends a little time on winding leafy lanes, past tea shops, pretty cottages and shops and follows ancient highways in the footsteps of the Romans.

From Elterwater, at the narrow mouth of Great Langdale, the main route straddles the shoulder of Loughrigg Fell before descending to Ambleside, that buzzing tourist centre on the northern shores of Lake Windermere. The lake itself is seen to good vantage from Jenkins Crag on an old road linking Ambleside and Troutbeck. The route climbs over the Garburn Pass into peaceful Kentmere, a village sitting pretty in peaceful pastures beneath the craggy peaks of the High Street range.

Those wishing to stick to the 'tops' are offered an itinerary which climbs to Loughrigg Fell and Wansfell Pike with the added bonus of a walk through a wooded dene to see the waterfalls of Stockghyll Force.

Opposite: Lake Windermere from Jenkin Crag. Below: Kentmere in the golden light of early morning.

ELTERWATER TO KENTMERE
The Main Route

ELTERWATER
The Ambleside road is followed out of the village past the rolling greens of Elterwater Common, turning right along the B road for a few hundred yards, then first left along a minor lane past the trees of Low Wood. Take the signposted footpath crossing the fields north of Loughrigg Tarn to reach a lane adjacent to a caravan and camping site.

LOUGHRIGG FELL
The path continues from the opposite side of the lane past a wood to exit at a stony track at GR 348042. This climbs past woods and continues by a wall (R) at the foot of bracken-clad flanks of Ivy Crag, a southern outlier of Loughrigg Fell.

The well-defined path then veers to the left (northeastwards) at the far end of some cultivated pastures, and, a short while afterwards, climbs to open fellsides. At GR 356043 there is a crossroads of paths by a small pool. Continue straight ahead to reach a gate in a dry stone wall.

AMBLESIDE
By now Ambleside has appeared beneath the expansive

Lake Windermere from Skelghyll Wood above Ambleside.

Around Ambleside

Ambleside has a long history. The Romans settled here and the remains of their fort, Galava, are to be found at Waterhead on the north-east side of Lake Windermere. The masonry has long since disappeared, robbed by generations of farmers for their walls and buildings.

The town is largely Victorian and grew from the rich pickings of tourism. In those early days visitors would arrive in Windermere by rail, take a steamer trip across the lake to Waterhead and then by carriage on the turnpike road into Ambleside itself.

Ambleside's oldest buildings are clustered around the Kirkstone Road. Here cobbled alleys run off a narrow twisting lane cramped by the hill slopes of Wansfell and Red Screes. Streams gush down steep fellsides. Once they powered water wheels for local corn mills. There is a restored wheel by Stock Beck near the North Road. Nearby is Bridge House, a tiny sixteenth century dwelling built over Stock Beck. At one time this area was cloaked by an orchard and the building was used as a storehouse for apples. Since then it has been a tea room, a cobbler's, a gift shop and now a National Trust information centre.

Poet William Wordsworth, synonymous with this part of Lakeland, had an office, The Old Stamp House, next to the old bakery on the corner of Church Street and Lake Road.

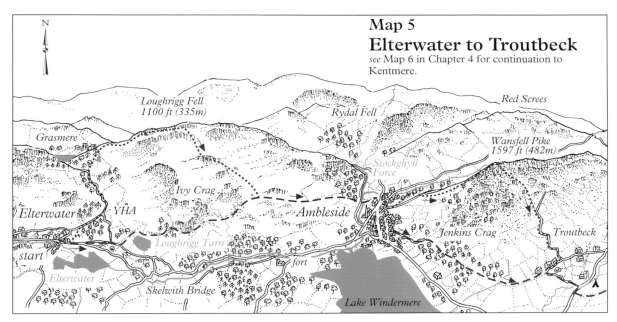

Map 5
Elterwater to Troutbeck
see Map 6 in Chapter 4 for continuation to Kentmere.

flanks of Wansfell. The prominent path descends north-eastwards before turning to the right to pass the southern edge of Deer Hows Wood. A twisting stony track then leads past more woodland to a metalled lane at Brow Head Farm. This descends to a minor road by the River Rothay, which is crossed via a footbridge. Here we can stroll into the heart of bustling Ambleside via Rothay Park.

After following the southbound street from Ambleside's centre, take the narrow lane from GR 377037, climbing the lower slopes of Wansfell above Lake Windermere.

JENKIN CRAG

A signposted track then leads into Skelghyll Wood to Jenkin Crag, which is a slight diversion to the right of the track. From this lofty perch there are views over the lake towards the fells of Coniston and Langdale but you will

probably have to share them for this is a busy little place.

TROUTBECK

The track continues out of the woods to high pastures, passing High Skelghyll Farm and contouring round the hillslopes high above Windermere. You can see down

Passing through Troutbeck.

Climbing from the valley at Troutbeck to Garburn Pass in the High Street range .

the length of the lake which lazes in very green and pleasant surroundings.

The track finally descends past some charming cottages and into Troutbeck. This tranquil village is tucked away from the main road in a tight and verdant valley shaded by the peaks of Yoke, Ill Bell and Froswick.

On leaving Troutbeck, take the lane opposite the post office across the river to the main road. A short distance along it to the south follow a stony track winding steeply uphill. The track soon assumes a north-easterly direction across Applethwaite Common. Ignore a prominent track beyond a gate to the left – this is the course of High Street, the Roman Road which skirts the sides of Yoke and Ill Bell to Thornthwaite Crag and eventually Penrith. As height is gained views down the valley to the Kirkstone Pass and Stony Cove Pike widen and become more impressive. In retrospect Lake Windermere is seen to good vantage, its blue waters stretching to the green fields, forests and undulating hills of southern Lakeland.

THE GARBURN PASS

On reaching the shoulder of the fell we have a decision to make – whether to follow the main 'pass' route or tackle the mountain route without dropping down to Kentmere. Unless it is well before lunch a wild campsite

will be necessary for the mountain route – the nearest accommodation at Bampton Grange is 13 miles (22km) away. If the weather is settled, however, the sunsets from the High Street ridge across the Lakeland peaks can be spectacular and well worth the effort (*see* Chapter 4 for route details).

KENTMERE

On the main route the stony track descends the rugged hillslopes in the shadow of Buck Crag and Ewe Crags. The cottages of Kentmere village are scattered below amid flat emerald fields which recede to the undulating countryside of southern Lakeland.

Kentmere Hall, seen to the right, was built onto a fourteenth-century pele tower. It was once home to Bernard Gilpin, who became Archdeacon of Durham and a leader of the Reformation. He was known as the Apostle of the North and was lucky to escape being burnt at the stake for his criticism of the Catholic Church. He broke his leg on his way to trial but in his convalescence Queen Mary died and was replaced by Protestant Queen Elizabeth I. There is a bronze memorial to him in the village church.

After passing The Nook (farm), a winding lane leads through the village, which has a post office, tea shop, B&B and church. St Cuthbert's church is sited on

Above: On the summit of Loughrigg Fell. Right: Stockghyll Force.

the foundations of an older church where St Cuthbert's body rested on its way to burial at Durham. We pass a few places which claim this; perhaps I should have called the route St Cuthbert's Carcass Way? Well, perhaps not.

GREAT LANGDALE TO KENTMERE
The Mountain Route

HIGH CLOSE
From the youth hostel at High Close, descend along the lane towards Grasmere then along the leafy track from GR 340056 through woodland. The track reaches the grassy flanks of Loughrigg Terrace high above Grasmere (lake). From here there are views across Grasmere village to Dunmail Raise, which is sandwiched between Steel Fell and Seat Sandal.

LOUGHRIGG FELL
Loughrigg Fell crowds us to the right. The popular path from here makes a direct assault but has some ghastly steps built into it – some improvement! There

Ambleside from the slopes of Wansfell Pike.

Kirkstone Pass. The path off Wansfell Pike descends eastwards to meet an enclosed track, Nanny Lane. This descends further to Troutbeck, where we once again meet the main route.

NB From Ambleside there is a mountain route for experienced fellwalkers intending to camp on high. Climb the spur of Snarker Pike to Red Screes summit then scramble down the path to the Kirkstone Pass. From there gain the High Street range via St Ravens Edge and Stony Cove Pike. There is a brief but steep drop to Threshthwaite Mouth before gaining Thornthwaite Beacon,where the mountain route from Kentmere is joined (*see* Chapter 4). Distance from Ambleside to Thornthwaite Beacon – *6 miles (10km).*

are no difficulties, however – follow the crowds south-eastwards on undulating terrain to the trig point, which has commanding views down the length of Lake Windermere to Morecambe Bay.

From the summit continue on the well-defined path south-eastwards passing a small tarn before descending to a marshy area, known as Black Mire, where the path heads first west then south to meet the main route at a crossroads of paths by a small pool (GR 356043). (Turn left then see previous description for the route to Ambleside.)

AMBLESIDE AND STOCKGHYLL FORCE

To keep faith with the high peak theme leave Ambleside by the lane signposted to Stock Ghyll. A footpath to the left then heads through pleasant woods to the waterfalls. Here, deep in the woods, two cascades join forces, plunging to a deep and turbulent pool.

Retrace your steps for a short way then take the higher path, which leads to an ornate metal gate by the lane. Turn left up the lane then abandon it for a footpath signposted to Wansfell Pike. This heads across fields with interesting views back to Ambleside and its surrounding fells.

WANSFELL PIKE AND TROUTBECK

The gradients become steeper and the path becomes an eroded scar in the upper flanks of the fell. The top is an airy place with good distant views down Great Langdale and also to the the High Street range and

ROUTE FILE

MAIN ROUTE

Distance	10 miles (17 km)
Time	6 hours
Terrain	Easy paths and quiet lanes across lowland terrain of riverside and pasture
Escape Routes	None required
Accommodation	Many inns and B&Bs at Ambleside. Inn and campsite at Troutbeck
Shops	P.O. and many shops at Ambleside P.O/general store at Troutbeck.

MOUNTAIN ROUTE

Distance	12 miles (18 km)
Time	7 hours
Terrain	Relatively easy paths with steep climbs over Loughrigg Fell and Wansfell
Escape Routes	None required
Accommodation	As main route
Shops	As main route

4

HIGH STREET AND MARDALE

Kentmere to Bampton Grange

Our last day in the Lake District is spent on the High Street fells which offers some of the pleasantest walking of the whole walk. The main route heads down the valley of Kentmere with the vegetated cliffs of Yoke, Ill Bell and Froswick glowering down on the green slopes surrounding Kentmere Reservoir.

At the valley head a fine zig-zag path climbs to the Nan Bield Pass, which is tightly tucked between the wild, rocky peaks of Harter Fell and Mardale Ill Bell at over 2,000 ft (600m) above sea level.

We're really in amongst the mountains now and we follow a twisting stony path past the isolated Small Tarn with majestic end-on views of Haweswater stretching to the horizon. The final stages along the western shorelines of Haweswater to Bampton Grange are as delightful as they are easy but it is with regret that we say goodbye to Lakeland.

The mountain alternative route is as good as any in Lakeland. Climbing to Yoke from the Garburn Pass, it continues on the craggy, conical hills of Ill Bell and Froswick before sampling splendid ridge routes over High Street, the Straights of Riggindale and High Raise. It almost seems a shame to come down but we eventually descend to the shores of Haweswater and the main route.

Harter Fell and the southern tip of Haweswater. The main route traces the far shores of the lake while the high route keeps to the skyline.

KENTMERE TO BAMPTON GRANGE
The Main Route

KENTMERE

A walled track from the east side of the church takes us out of the village. After a third of a mile (500m), at GR 460046, the track is abandoned for a path to the right, which crosses the River Kent by a footbridge before climbing westwards to another walled track known as Low Lane. A left turn is made along the lane to Overend, which lies at the terminus of a metalled lane from the village. From here the cultivated fields of Kentmere are surrounded by shapely fells on three sides. Rainsbarrow Crag and Tongue Scar form a narrow neck around the lower valley pastures, squeezing them to the sliver of green ringed by the cliffs of Ill Bell and Froswick and the crag-fringed peaks of Mardale Ill Bell and Harter Fell.

Beyond Overend Farm the higher more easterly bridleway is followed through fields beneath woodland and the craggy facade of Withered Howe. Further north, beneath the spur of Tongue Scar (not marked on 1:50,000 maps but just north-east of the ruins of Tongue House), the path turns to the left through a

Above: Descending from Nan Bield to Haweswater. Below: Ill Bell and Froswick from Kentmere.

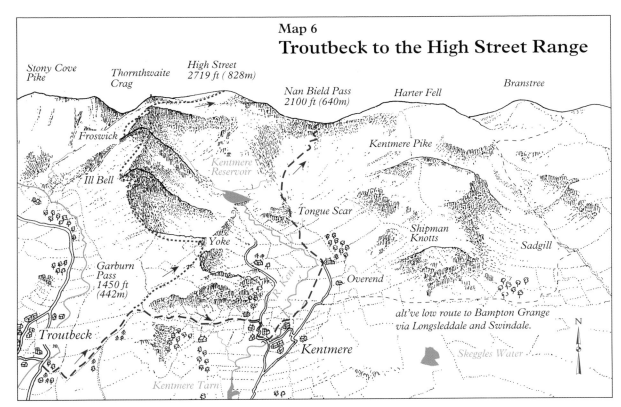

Map 6

Troutbeck to the High Street Range

Stony Cove Pike

Thornthwaite Crag

High Street 2719 ft (828m)

Nan Bield Pass 2100 ft (640m)

Harter Fell

Branstree

Froswick

Kentmere Reservoir

Kentmere Pike

Ill Bell

Tongue Scar

Shipman Knotts

Sadgill

Yoke

Garburn Pass 1450 ft (442m)

Overend

alt've low route to Bampton Grange via Longsleddale and Swindale.

Troutbeck

Kentmere

Skeggles Water

Kentmere Tarn

N

gate in the dry-stone wall and over a shallow stream. It then tackles Tongue Scar. The Kentmere Reservoir soon comes into view beneath the steep craggy ramparts of Ill Bell and Yoke. It is an impressive scene slightly marred by the quarries close to the dam.

NAN BIELD PASS

Ahead of us is Mardale Ill Bell. It sends out a grassy spur, Lingmell End, which plummets to the reservoir shores. Our path keeps to the east of the spur and zigzags up grassy slopes, which become more rocky as height is gained. Soon we are at a high pass, Nan Bield. A good stone shelter offers respite from hostile conditions.

From Nan Bield it's nearly all downhill for the day. A winding stony track threads through craggy knolls and bouldered slopes with two lakes clearly visible. The higher is Small Water, a tear-shaped tarn, cradled by crags: the other is Haweswater, a four-mile long enlarged lake which now fills the beautiful Mardale Valley (*see* box). Only the southern finger is visible as yet.

After rounding the northern shores of Small Water, the path continues its descent close to the banks of its

outflowing stream. The boisterous waters descend a rocky ravine in a series of cataracts and falls. With each step we take a little more of Haweswater is revealed. The cliff face of Harter Fell to the right is also becoming more impressive. In views to the left the dark crags of the summit cap of High Street peep over the lower corrie of Blea Water Beck. This bustling stream joins forces with Small Water Beck to feed the ever-hungry waters of Haweswater.

HAWESWATER

As our route nears the lake and road terminus we turn left on another path signposted 'to Bampton'. This beautiful route takes us round to the western shorelines of Haweswater. If you are lucky you might catch sight of a golden eagle in flight, for this rare and protected species nests hereabouts. The well-defined path climbs to fields above the conifer forest cloaking the isthmus known as the Rigg. It then descends into Riggindale, a deep chasm crowded beneath the crag-crested flanks of Kidsty Pike and Riggindale Crags. After crossing its stream the path veers north-eastwards, parallel to the

The Sinking of Mardale

Mardale was a small pastoral valley, perhaps most famed for its butter and milk. William Wordsworth likened its lake, Haweswater to a 'lesser Ullswater': the surrounding fellsides are certainly very similar in nature. The lake had natural beaches where primroses fringed the banks. Its village, Mardale Green, consisted of a pub, the Dun Bull, a church surrounded by yew trees and some whitewashed cottages. In his *Coast to Coast* book, A. Wainwright reminisced of hedgerows sweet with flowers and wild roses.

That was before 1937 when the Manchester Water Authority constructed a massive 120ft (360m)concrete dam, to raise the water level by 96ft (30m) and which would flood much of the upper valley. Last orders were called at the Old Dun Bull; the cobbler and shopkeepers closed their doors and Mardale Green was lost forever, submerged by this great wall of water.

Yes, life in the valley was silenced to feed the noisy pistons of industry. Occasionally quiet reminders of the past come to light when, after periods of draught, the water-level drops to reveal the skeletons of vegetation and the village's foundations and dry-stone walls, crumbling amidst the crazed mozaic of drying mud. Probably a little of the spirit lives on in nearby Bampton.

Old photographs of village and valley can be seen in the Haweswater Hotel, halfway along the road that runs along the eastern shores of the reservoir.

lake shore. Be careful not to be enticed onto the well-used route climbing to Kidsty Pike.

Randale Beck is crossed by way of a footbridge and the path climbs slightly left before resuming its north-easterly course along the bottom edge of a small copse. It then climbs (unmercifully so late in the day) to Flakehowe Crags (not named on Landranger maps) beneath Birks Crag. This lofty perch gives full value for the effort spent however, for it offers lovely views down the length of Haweswater and the verdant patchwork landscapes of the Lowther Valley.

Descending once more to cross Whelter Beck our route traverses the boulder fields beneath the crags of

Right: Haweswater: late sunshine breaks through the rain clouds.

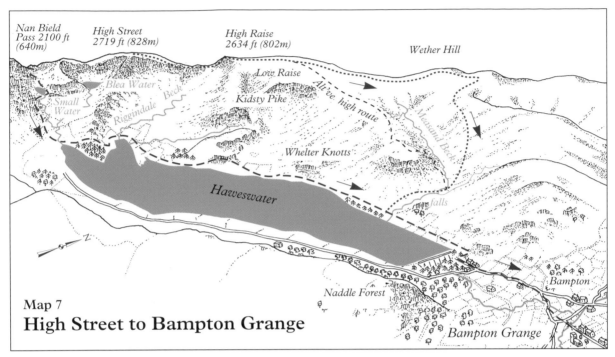

Nan Bield Pass 2100 ft (640m)

High Street 2719 ft (828m)

High Raise 2634 ft (802m)

Wether Hill

Blea Water

Low Raise

Alt've high route

Measand Beck

Small Water

Kidsty Pike

Riggindale Beck

Whelter Knotts

falls

Haweswater

Naddle Forest

Bampton

Bampton Grange

Map 7
High Street to Bampton Grange

Benty Howe. A mile and a half (2.5km) further on we cross the footbridge over Measand Beck. It is well worth a short exploration uphill for the river, which keeps its secrets well hidden, powerfully cascades through deep, tree-fringed, rocky ravines. Further along the shores our path meets a wide track leading past the huge concrete reservoir dam to Burnbanks. Country lanes should then be followed to the fine twin-arched bridge over Haweswater Beck.

BAMPTON GRANGE

The village of Bampton Grange (inn) is reached via a cross-field footpath which begins from the ladder stile adjacent to the small chapel on the opposite banks of the beck.

NB The village of Bampton also has some accommodation (an inn and a campsite) on offer. It can be reached from the previously mentioned bridge over Haweswater Beck by following the footpath along the west banks of the river and thence by quiet country lanes.

Approaching Bampton Grange from the bridge over Haweswater Beck.

KENTMERE TO BAMPTON GRANGE
A Mountain Route

KENTMERE

On reaching a bend in the track (GR 435044) just short of the Garburn Pass, the mountain alternative leaves the wide track for a faint path heading northwards across a stretch of marshy grassland for the mountains.

YOKE

It eventually makes for the crest of the ridge. The ridge wall is then followed on a dull plod towards the summit of Yoke. The very top of this fell is circumvented to the left (west). Once beyond it, the prospects improve and we can see down the shattered crags above Rainsbarrow Cove into the depths of Upper Kentmere, where the solemn waters lie cradled by the stark, scaly slopes of Kentmere Common and Harter Fell.

ILL BELL AND FROSWICK

Our next peak, Ill Bell, rises up from the col like a rough rocky pyramid. It looks and is in every sense a true mountain. A good mountain path climbs by the cliff edge to its diminutive summit, which is crowned by some tall stone cairns.

I have just read in the *Great Outdoors* magazine that two walkers were seen flattening the main cairn. When asked why they decreed that cairns had no place among the mountains. Although it is true that in some places there is a proliferation of ill-placed modern walkers' cairns and they do little for the scene, this one was over 200 years old. Do these people intend to go for other historical features that dare to be sited on *their* mountains – the Roman forts at Hardknott or Chew Green perhaps?

Views back to Yoke reveal a new and more dramatic side to its character for it now boasts some tremendous cliffs, which plummet to the green fields of Kentmere. Ahead lies a lower peak, cheekily mimicking Ill Bell. This young pretender is Froswick. Our route from Ill Bell descends north-westwards down rocky flanks with steep drops northwards down Over Cove. The path gradually changes to a northerly direction at the col then boldly climbs Froswick.

From Froswick we can see more intimately the colossus of the main High Street massif. rearing up from behind Thornthwaite Crag, whose 15ft (4.5m)

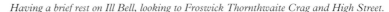

Having a brief rest on Ill Bell, looking to Froswick Thornthwaite Crag and High Street.

On Rampsgill Head with Kidsty Pike and Haweswater in the distance.

stone beacon can clearly be seen. A wide and wild coombe at the head of Kentmere is ringed by the steep slopes of Gavel Crag, Mardale Ill Bell and the grassy spur of Lingmell End.

HIGH STREET
A north-westerly descent is made from Froswick on a narrow path to the col.

After climbing on the lower slopes of Thornthwaite Crag the route divides. The left fork heads for Thornthwaite Beacon. We want the right fork – the course of the old Roman Road known as High Street. The ancient byway, which has climbed the fellsides from Troutbeck, is followed north-eastwards above Gavel Crag towards High Street (the mountain). Make for the terminus of the ridge wall to the east of Thornthwaite Crag and thence follow the line of dilapidated fence posts to reach the main High Street ridge wall. The wall is now followed to the summit.

This place was once known as Racecourse Hill, a name dating back to the times when the locals from the village of Mardale Green used to congregate here for an annual festival, which included horse racing. The same horses were also used to carry ale and provisions for the revelry.

Views of the surrounding corries are obscured by the expansive plateau and, if time is unimportant, detours would be rewarded. The view from the western edge reveals the beautifully sculpted hollow of Hayeswater, whose large lake is surrounded by precipitous slopes and screes of the Knott and the narrow shapely spur of Gray Crag. The exquisite situation of Blea Water is best viewed from the cliff edges to the north-east of the summit. The lake is set deep into a circular basin bounded by the cliff fringes of Rough Crag and the rocky bluffs of Mardale Ill Bell. Harter Fell and a finger of Haweswater form the backdrop to this rich tapestry.

High Street's ridge wall is followed northwards above the clifftops, descending to the Straits of Riggindale. Here Kidsty Pike dominates the scene, its crags sitting high above grassy ramparts which sweep to the depths of Riggindale, another deep hollow at the head of Haweswater. The path divides at the foot of

Rampsgill Head. The one to the left (to be avoided) heads for the Knott and descends to Hartsop and Brotherswater. It would offer a good escape route for those caught in hostile conditions.

RAMPSGILL HEAD
Our route follows the path to the right, climbing to Rampsgill Head. Retrospective views to High Street and Riggindale Crags are spectacular and memorable. In mist be careful not to be lured onto the well used 'Coast-to-Coast' path eastwards to Kidsty Pike. Our route continues north-eastwards at the head of Martindale. This gigantic hollow is part of a deer park and out of bounds to walkers, which is a shame for it looks to be a fascinating place. I am informed that the deer sometimes roam onto the ridges hereabouts though I have never actually seen one.

HIGH RAISE
After dropping to a minor pass there is a simple ascent to the High Street range's second highest peak, High Raise. Its airy summit gives excellent views in all directions. Beyond the huge scoop of Martindale many of the Lake District's highest mountains are included in a superb panorama. Dominant amongst these are the Fairfield and Helvellyn ranges, Skiddaw, Blencathra, Bowfell and Crinkle Crags. To the east the pale outlines of the highest Pennines, including Cross Fell, the Howgills and Wild Boar Fell, fill the skyline beyond the commons of Mardale and Shap. To the north the undulating peaty tops of the High Street ridge decline gently towards the anonymity of the Lowther and Eamont Valleys.

There are two routes from High Raise to Measand Beck and the shores of Haweswater. The first is a bridleway (the Roman road) which descends northwards to a ridge wall and continues to the summit of Wether Fell. From here a path doubles back down High Kop to the old quarries at Low Kop then rakes down steep grassy slopes to the bridge over Measand Beck (GR483157).

A second more logical route from High Raise (but not strictly a right of way) leaves the well-trodden Lakeland highways behind and heads ENE on a narrow path to Low Raise. From here the paths are little more than sheep-tacks. Haweswater is seen to good vantage for the first time when the route reaches Bason Crag.

All traces of a path are lost north of here and it is best to round the coombe then head north-eastwards

down the rough, grassy slopes north of Laythwaite Crags. If visibility is good, head in the direction of the white radar dome which crowns Great Dun Fell on the horizon.

MEASAND BECK FALLS
If you get your bearings right you will come across a grooved track, which zig-zags down the steep flanks of Measand End. Otherwise make your own way down to the previously mentioned footbridge.

HAWESWATER
A right of way, unclear underfoot, now descends to Haweswater but most walkers follow more closely the stream which cascades spectacularly over crags and through rocky ravines. The main route is met at a footbridge spanning the beck just above the lakeshore and a left turn is made following the path via Burnbanks and thence on country lanes to Bampton Grange (see previous description).

ROUTE FILE
Main Route

Distance	12 miles (19 km)
Time	7 hours
Terrain	Well defined mountain paths
Accommodation	B&B at Bampton and Bampton Grange. Also (off route) the Haweswater Hotel on the eastern shores of Haweswater. Wild camp sites around Small Water above Mardale
shops	P.O. at Bampton and Bampton Grange

Mountain Route

Distance	15 miles (23 km)
Time	9 hours
Terrain	Well defined mountain paths to High Raise then pathless, grassy ridges down to Haweswater
Escape Routes	From Thornthwaite Crag or the Knott down to Hartsop via Hayeswater
Accommodation	Many good wild camping sites on the ridges and lake filled corries plus Bampton/Bampton Grange
Shops	as main route

5

LEAVING THE LAKES FOR THE GARDEN OF EDEN

Bampton Grange to Temple Sowerby

Leaving the beauty and grandeur of the lakes behind is hard, especially when the map promises us relatively flat country around the plains of the Eden Valley.

All is not lost, however, for the Eden Valley is well named. This peaceful and picturesque garden is embellished with charming villages, quiet country lanes and lazy, meandering streams and rivers. Birds sing from hedgerows and tree-tops and we are assured that God is in his Heaven.

From Bampton Grange the route climbs the limestone escarpment of Out Scar before traversing the flat fields and forests of the Lowther Estate. This is as high as it gets today unless you make one supreme effort to scale Cross Fell.

After a last look back at Mardale, the route descends to cross the busy M6 motorway (by a bridge of course). We are now in low-lying agricultural lands. A series of winding country lanes and field paths lead through Morland before meeting the wide River Eden. An idyllic riverside path leads lazily into Temple Sowerby, a pleasing village with charming cottages strung around a huge tree-lined green.

Opposite: Measand Beck Falls seen on the shore path along Haweswater. Below: Relaxing by the green at Temple Sowerby.

BAMPTON GRANGE TO TEMPLE SOWERBY
The Main Route

Out Scar - a pastoral scene seen early in the day.

BAMPTON GRANGE
The eastbound lane out of Bampton Grange is followed past Field Gate House then abandoned at a sharp corner (GR 529183) for a path which heads for Out Scar on the southern edge of the Lowther Park Estate.

OUT SCAR AND LOWTHER PARK
The route is unclear underfoot. Ignore the prominent track which eventually heads northwards. Instead strike ENE across the field and you will locate a well-hidden ladder stile after passing between some bushes. Aim for the top right-hand corner of the next large field, go through the gate, follow the course of the wall to the left. This leads to the ruins of Scarside, which are circumvented to the left.

Continuing across a field we then enter the gorse-scattered environs of Knipescar Common. Looking back we have a wonderful panorama of the Lakeland Fells, the High Street Range being most prominent. A corner of Haweswater can be seen beyond the village of Bampton Grange, which hugs the winding banks of the River Lowther.

A gate in tall stone walls allows entry into the high fields of Out Scar on the Lowther Estate. No path

Passing through the picturesque village of Morland.

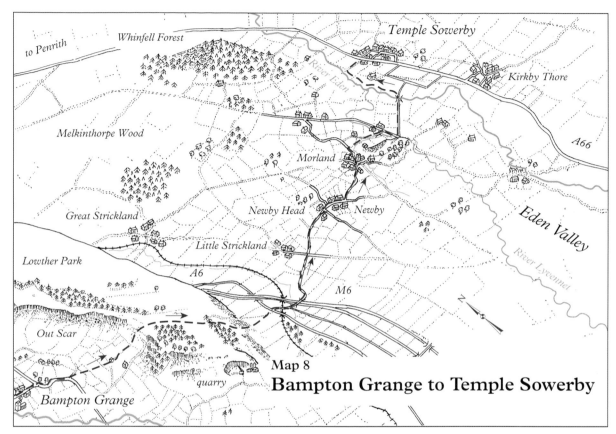

Map 8
Bampton Grange to Temple Sowerby

exists underfoot. A bearing of 77degrees (ENE) will lead you past the grassed-over quarry workings at the top of the hill. The route continues eastwards, close to conifer plantations (on the right) to the gate at the western edge of the Shapbeck Gate plantation. A large quarry will be seen to the south.

CROSSING THE M6
A track leads eastwards through the woods and this is followed by a trek across two fields to the busy A6 highway. This is crossed and the minor lane opposite is followed over the M6 to the adjoining villages of Newby Head and Newby. Farm tracks run parallel to the road but that route would be more circuitous.

MORLAND
A left turn at Newby leads into Morland. The village is a cluster of charming cottages surrounding a pretty sandstone church. The church, which has a blue clock on its three-storey tower, has Norman origins and

includes some fine carved oak. By its gate stands a Spanish chestnut tree with a trunk as thick as I have seen. It seems a shame to pass through Morland without further exploration but press on we must.

The road past the church is followed northwards out of the village. After half a mile (800m), a bridleway to the right, marked 'to Crossriggs' leads north-eastwards by a brook, passing a delightfully situated white-washed cottage, Glenton Vale, on the opposite bank. A short way beyond the cottage the path veers away from the stream for a while. At GR 602236 it meets a bridleway by a footbridge spanning the brook.

The hedge-lined track heads north-eastwards to meet a wider farm track, which then leads northwards. A right turn at a T-junction takes us along a farm track past Winter House. Here a rutted track beyond a red gate is followed over the bridge across the River Lyvennet, a tributary of the Eden. It continues past Crossriggs Hall to the road, where a right turn is made. Turn left at the next junction on a northbound country lane passing the cottage of Ousen Stand to a fine bridge over the River Eden.

BY THE BANKS OF THE EDEN

The lanes are thankfully abandoned for a path along the north-eastern banks of the river. A five-bar gate to the left on the far side of the bridge gives us access and the riverbanks are followed by a fence. Beyond a stream-crossing climb to higher banks near the old Temple Sowerby Station, now converted into a house. The path passes close to the abutments of the old rail-

The River Eden at Temple Sowerby.

way bridge and past Skygarth Farm. Turn right beyond an old kissing gate preceding a bend in the river.

TEMPLE SOWERBY

Hereabouts the path climbs steeply up a grassy bank to a gate with a way-marking arrow, then continues north-eastwards on a narrow enclosed track to the outskirts of Temple Sowerby and the A66, which does its best without quite succeeding to dissect the village. A short way south along the road is a Roman milestone.

As we make our way to the village centre it is easy to understand why Temple Sowerby is known as the Queen of Westmorland Villages. A huge green, lined with sycamore and lime, separates the many seventeenth century cottages, grand Georgian houses and sandstone church of the village. Until the middle of this century the carefully mown green was more of a meadow, flower-filled and grazed by cattle and geese.

If you started the day at Bampton then this will be a short day. However the choice of accommodation is wider here than in many of the surrounding place and only the strongest of walkers could make it to Garrigill.

Acorn Bank and The Knights Templar

Temple Sowerby's early history, including its name, is rooted in the Knights Templar, who resided at Sowerby Manor, now known as Acorn Bank. (We will pass this tomorrow.)

The Knights were soldiers who had taken religious vows and were devoted to the fight against Saracens and non-Christians. In 1323 the manor was passed to the Knights of St. John of Jerusalem. Henry VIII disbanded this group during the dissolution of the monasteries and the Sowerby Hall estate was given to the Dalstons, who renamed it Acorn Bank. The building was heavily renovated in the eighteenth century.

A later owner of the house was authoress Dorothy Una Ratcliffe. She and her husband restored the neglected house to its former glory before presenting it to the National Trust in 1950. The trust planted and designed an impressive herb garden with many of the plants used in medieval and modern medicine.

In 1976 the Sue Ryder Foundation converted the building itself to a home for elderly and disabled people.

The village itself grew from its position on the Penrith-Darlington turnpike road, then the railway. It became an important cattle and trading centre with four annual fairs and a profitable tanning business. The maypole opposite what is now the Temple Sowerby Hotel was once the site of a traditional 'lying competition' in which the first prize was a grindstone to keep a sharp wit. It is said that a bishop came to condemn the ceremony stating that he had never told a lie in his life. He was unanimously given first prize.

ROUTE FILE

Distance	10 miles (16 km)
Time	5 hours
Terrain	Very easy day on country lanes, and footpaths by the riverside and across fields
Accommodation	Inn and B&B at Morland. Inn, hotel and B&B at Temple Sowerby
Shops	P.O./general store and butcher at Temple Sowerby.

6

SCALING THE HIGHEST PENNINES

Temple Sowerby to Garrigill

After a brief wander through the fields of Eden our route makes a welcome return to the mountains.

From Temple Sowerby pleasant paths descend to the beautiful gardens of Acorn Bank and into the sylvan dene of Crowdundle Brook. The stream has flowed from the lofty North Pennine peaks that fringe the horizon. They get nearer with every step.

Country lanes continue through Blencarn to Kirkland, a village lying right at the foot of Cross Fell, which at 2930ft (893m) is the highest Pennine. A well-graded track climbs to the saddle at the northern foot of Cross Fell, where we have a choice of routes. The main route continues on the old track, descending past the old lead mines to Garrigill in the verdant South Tyne Valley. Alternatively the high route climbs to Cross Fell's summit to view a full 360 degree panorama of the hills and plains of Lakeland, the Northern Pennines and the Scottish Borders. The route continues along the high ridge to Great Dun Fell, where it descends via Trout Beck. This seldom-trod path through vast and remote hillscapes passes the source of the River South Tyne before meeting the main route at Garrigill.

Descending on the high route from Great Dun Fell by Dunfell Hush with Cow Green Reservoir in the distance beyond vast spartan moors.

TEMPLE SOWERBY TO GARRIGILL
The Main Route

TEMPLE SOWERBY

A footpath between houses at the east side of the village green and signposted 'to the Newbiggin Road' is followed across meadows. After going through a kissing gate the path follows a hedge to the left consisting of blackthorn, elder, hazel, wild roses and crab-apples. Smoke will probably be seen coming from the Kirkby Thore gypsum works to the right while, from the top of the field, Cross Fell dominates the view ahead across wide pastureland.

ACORN BANK

On reaching the road, a left turn is made to the junction with Tanyard Lane (GR 613279). Turn right here on a path across fields on a slight ridge before crossing Birk Sike via a small footbridge. The path continues north-eastwards, passing to the left of Acorn Bank's house and car park (*see* box, Chapter 5).

Behind the house the path descends through a gate into the woods to Crowdundle Beck. The scene is particularly pleasant in spring when snowdrops, daffodils and primroses appear amid rowan, spindle and crab-apple trees. Bird life is abundant. You may well see a kingfisher or heron and are very likely to see pied wagtails, dippers and tits.

The path passes a footbridge (do not cross) then beneath a four-arched, red sandstone viaduct conveying the Settle to Carlisle railway. If you are lucky you might see one of the classic steam trains of yesteryear, for they are often used at weekends and holiday times on this line.

NEWBIGGIN HALL

The path emerges at the road just to the north of Newbiggin Hall (private house). This splendid sandstone building has two castellated towers which were rebuilt for the Crackenthorpe family in the sixteenth century. Originally the towers had life-size soldiers in armour on the battlements. The house was bought by William and Dorothy Cookson (herself a Crackenthorpe) the grandparents of lakeland poet, William Wordsworth. The hall and neighbouring church underwent further modification in the late eighteenth century.

The road, which is followed to the left, crosses the beck then zig-zags up the hill past Scar Top. A right turn is made at the first junction and the pleasant tree-enshrouded lane leads past Blencarn Village then past its lake.

On a pretty country lane near Blencarn.

KIRKLAND

The lane continues to the hamlet of Kirkland dominated by the soaring slopes of Cross Fell.

Continue to the right of the old church on a narrow metalled lane past some pleasant cottages. The lane degenerates into a stony track and crosses Kirkland Beck before winding up the hillside round the crags of High Cap.

Resist the urge to cut the corner for no time will be saved and a lot of valuable effort will have been wasted.

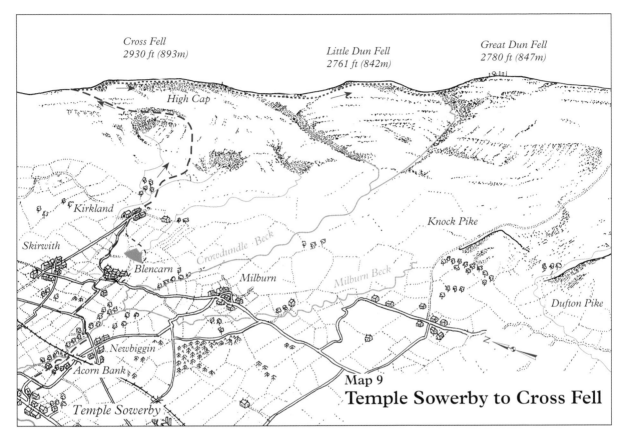

Cross Fell
2930 ft (893m)

Little Dun Fell
2761 ft (842m)

Great Dun Fell
2780 ft (847m)

High Cap

Kirkland

Skirwith

Blencarn

Milburn

Crowdundle Beck

Milburn Beck

Knock Pike

Dufton Pike

Newbiggin

Acorn Bank

Temple Sowerby

Map 9
Temple Sowerby to Cross Fell

Some disused pits, now largely grassed over, are passed and the track becomes a cairned path. The course is never in doubt however, even in the mist. Soon the bouldered upper slopes of Cross Fell come into view across the wild grassy shoulder of the fellsides. We are now on the expansive watershed. It is here that we must make the choice of whether or not to use the mountain route. (*See* Mountain Alternative for routes to Cross Fell).

GREG'S HUT

On descending to the flanks of Skirwith Fell, the terrain becomes more boulder-strewn and we come across an old stone cottage, Greg's Hut, lying in total isolation amidst a vast wilderness of rolling peat-clad hills. This old miners' dwelling was restored by the Mountain Bothies Association to offer shelter for weary travellers. If you use the hut make sure you clean up afterwards so that others can enjoy their stay.

The path enters an area littered by the debris, shafts and spoil heaps of the old disused lead mines. The

Greg's Hut, a remote bothy on the shoulder of Cross Fell.

Above: Descending into the South Tyne Valley with the cottages of Garrigill tucked beneath the hillsides. Below: A quiet corner of Garrigill.

ground is covered with purple crystalline pebbles of fluorospar or Blue John, a waste product of the mining.

Continuing past the mine-workings, the track veers northwards, passing Long Man Hill and Pikeman Hill. Views of the green swathes of the South Tyne Valley become wider as the long descent draws to a close.

GARRIGILL

Garrigill, which means Gerrard's Valley, lies in seclusion by the banks of the South Tyne and well away from the main Middleton to Alston road. This pleasant village has a large green, lined by old stone dwellings. Its growth probably stemmed from its nearness to the lead mines on

Map 10
Cross Fell to Garrigill

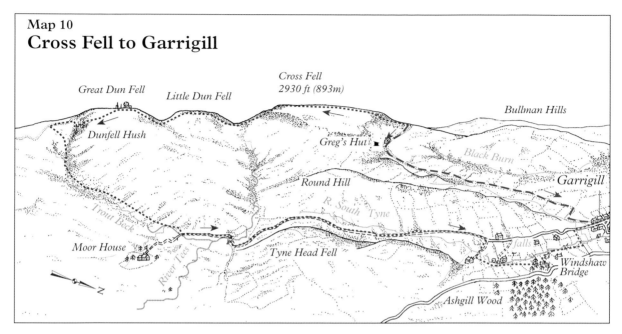

Cross Fell. The George and Dragon is a fine inn. Having often stayed there, I can thoroughly recommend the food and hospitality.

KIRKLAND TO GARRIGILL
A Mountain Alternative via Cross Fell

CROSS FELL
The main route is left on reaching the ridge north of Cross Fell. A track to the right clambers SSE up stony slopes to reach Cross Fell's summit, which is recognized by the cross-wall shelter and trig point. The plateau is quite extensive and consists of firm ground with short grass and scattered boulders. View are wide-reaching. The whole of the Lake District is paraded before your eyes beyond the pastures of Eden. Across the waters of the Solway Firth are the Galloway Hills, while to the east successive ridges of wild moorland pale to the Hexhamshire horizon.

It is southwards that we now go – our next two hills, the Little and Great Dun Fells are both plainly visible. The latter, as will have been seen for many miles, is dubiously decorated with the white dome and masts of a radar station. The blue lake seen in the distance to the south-east is the Cow Green Reservoir, built in the

1960s in the midst of tremendous controversy. Its site was considered an area of extreme scientific importance due to the rich diversity of alpine plant life on the sugar limestone fells.

On the edge of the plateau is a tall cairn marking the descent to Tees Head, where the river of that name is born. Unfortunately the 'path improvers' have been at work laying huge rock slabs over the fellsides between here and Great Dun Fell. It is almost as big an insult as the radar station and complete overkill for these hills are not that well walked and not that badly eroded.

LITTLE AND GREAT DUN FELLS
A short climb follows from Tees Head to Little Dun Fell, a narrow grassy diadem with good views back to the colossus that is Cross Fell.

Descend Little Dun Fell and climb the grassy slopes to Great Dun Fell.– no complications and not too much effort. There are more of those horrible slabs, though. Great Dun Fell is a mess and there will be no desire to linger beneath its masts. The path passes to the east side of them before descending to Dunfell Hush, a huge man-made ravine.

TROUT BECK
Cross Dunfell Hush and follow the path to the metalled approach road to the station at its junction with a stony

Cross Fell Lead Mines

On the traverse of the high Pennines one cannot help but notice the evidence of extensive mining on the fells – the artificial hushes on Knock Fell and Great Dun Fell and the shafts, debris and relics on the descent to Garrigill. The area is rich in lead, silver, iron, zinc and copper: all have been mined here.

It was lead that brought prosperity to the region. The Romans were first to discover it but their diggings were not extensive. Mining was resumed by the Earls of Derwentwater, but in 1716, the last Earl, James, was executed on Tower Hill for his part in the Jacobite rebellions. His lands were granted to the Greenwich Hospital who still own them to this day.

Horizontal passages (levels), some to ventilate and some to drain the mines, were dug. This resulted in many tons of unprofitable stone being strewn across the fellsides. Miners used the levels for easy access to the face and worked eight-hour shifts. This gave time for the harmful dust to settle.

The industry reached its peak during the eighteenth and nineteenth centuries when worked by the Quaker London Lead Company who rented the land from the Greenwich Hospital. They genuinely tried to improve the life of the miner and helped them to build small-holdings on hillsides near to the mines. They also subsidized libraries and schools.

It was still a very hard life, however, and, in the eighteenth century a miner could only expect to live to about thirty-five years of age. In 1842, figures produced showed that 88 out of Alston's 100 widows receiving Parish Relief had been lead miners' wives. After a General Board of Health Inspection in 1858 it was found that Alston had a higher proportion of widows than any other place in Britain and there was not a single miner whose sputum was not stained by the blue-black dust ingested during the working day. Life expectancy had increased by another ten years.

In 1882, the company sold their leases to the Nenthead and Tynehead Lead and Zinc company for £30,000 and by the end of the century mining on a large scale ceased. Most miners abandoned their uneconomic small-holdings, which were left to decay along with the mine-workings.

mine track (GR 716316). Descend along the coarse, stony track, which doubles back towards the hush. A grassy track then traces its southern edge eastwards down the fellsides.

Our track seeks out the beginnings of Trout Beck then degenerates into a path along its northern banks. The hillscapes are vast and as bleak as any encountered on the journey so far. Only the white walls of the distant Moor House break the theme.

MOOR HOUSE

In its lower reaches the path meets a track by a bridge next to a waterfall. The large building to the east of the bridge is English Nature's, Moor House, seen earlier and part of Britain's largest nature reserve. The surrounding hills, including Cross Fell, have been designated a Biosphere Reserve, part of a world-wide network of protected areas. The reserve largely consists of blanket bog up to four metres thick. Sphagnum moss, cotton grass and heather are the main constituents of the bog but 290 species of flowering plant, 260 mosses, 75 liverworts, 120 lichens and 40 algae also grow in the area.

Do not cross the bridge but stay with the track. downstream, Trout Beck feeds into the Tees, which has become a lot more mature since last we saw it. The famous river can be seen snaking across a wide brown moorland expanse with Cross Fell and the Dun Fells filling the horizon.

TYNE HEAD

The track crosses the Tees and turns left, climbing slightly to Tyne Head. (Ignore the track to the right, which heads for the mines of Metalband Hill.)

After descending slightly the track crosses the infant Tyne (coming from the right) very close to its source. It is amazing that two great rivers are born so close. The babbling stream accompanies the route through a wild and narrow valley littered with shakeholes and old mine workings. We are shaded by the slopes of Round Hill (left) and Tynehead Fell (right).

SOUTH TYNE VALLEY

The valley widens and pastured hill slopes can be seen in the view ahead. The river has also become more lively and rushes over its ore-stained rock bed.

Beyond Dorthgill farm, formerly known as Tea-Kettle Hall, the track passes to the right of an old lime kiln. Strange though it may seem in a limestone area, the soil is actually acid and local smallholders had to burn lime to spread over their cultivated enclosures.

Beyond the lime kiln the terminus of a country lane is met. This could be followed for the 3 miles (5km) into Garrigill but a more entertaining way would be to turn sharp right, descending to Tynehead farm. This was once part of an independent hamlet with its own Lord of the Manor. It is believed that there was a Roman settlement here. Behind Tynehead is a lovely small limestone gorge complete with a waterfall. This is the Clargill Burn. Just further upstream is a vein which was the best silver producer in the area, yielding 40oz (1kg) per ton of ore.

The South Tyne, now a glistening and lively trout-filled brook, is crossed by the house. A stile marks the start of a path northwards along the river, keeping to the right of Hole House Farm.

ASH GILL FORCE

There is a waterfall, Ashgill Force, well worth seeing at GR 757405. It is just a short distance east of the path and can be reached by following a concessionary path on the northern banks of Ash Gill just after the footbridge crossing. Locals say that fairies have been known to dance on the rocky shelf behind the plume of water.

GARRIGILL

After retracing your steps to the bridge, head for the banks of the South Tyne. Grass of Parnassus, a delicate white flower, primroses and the common spotted and fragrant orchids grow in the terraced fields hereabouts, while dippers mallards teals, goosanders and herons may also be seen.

Trace the banks of the Tyne to Windshaw Bridge, which should be crossed to gain the Garrigill Road at Crossgill, half a mile short of the village.

POSSIBLE ALTERNATIVES

Cross Fell can be tackled on the bridleway from Blencarn. For those who do not fancy the wiggle over Little and Great Dun Fells, the main route could be regained from Cross Fell by descending ENE along the

Descending the lonely North Pennine moors by the banks of Trout Beck.

summit plateau then following the fence down Fallow Hill. This meets the old corpse road at GR 710358.

ROUTE FILE

Main Route

Distance	14 miles (22 km)
Time	8 hours
Terrain	Easy level footpaths and country lanes followed by stony tracks and firm mountain paths on the shoulder of Cross Fell. Can be extremely trying when there is a Helm Wind. Reaches the highest ground encountered along the whole of the main route
Accommodation	George & Dragon Inn and B&Bs at Garrigill. Bothy at Greg's Hut north of Cross Fell for emergencies
Shops	P.O./general store at Garrigill

Mountain Route

Distance	19 miles (30 km)
Time	11 hours
Terrain	Tough and lengthy route over the highest Pennines taking the walker into very remote parts. Good navigational skills required and not recommended in unsettled weather
Escape Routes	1 If weather worsens on Cross Fell return to Greg's Hut. 2 As a last resort on or near Great Dun Fell locate the metalled lane and descend to to the village of Knock
Accommodation	As main route
Shops	As main route

7

OVER THE MOOR TO ALLENDALE

Garrigill to Allendale Town

On this day we leave Cumbria. While memories of high Lakeland still linger we can now look forward to Northumberland, its mountains and coastline.

On climbing out of the verdant South Tyne valley the route re-enters spartan moorland to reach Nenthead, a straggling village still entangled in its nineteenth century industrial past.

Beyond Nenthead we cross the county border. Northumberland begins savagely and the route traverses lofty heather moors past sombre ruins on a track ominously called the Black Way. As if to make amends the new county offers us teasing glimpses of green. East Allendale shyly presents itself and a descent is made to its lovely river.

Holm's Linn is a picturesque waterfall seen on a riverside stroll that equals that by the Eden. Narrow paths squeeze through riverside woodlands and over grassy knolls.

Finally we cross the river and enter Allendale Town, a proud village built from the profits of lead-mining.

Opposite: Holm's Linn waterfalls in East Allendale. Below: Nenthead from the north-east.

Garrigill to Allendale Town
The Main Route

This day begins and ends with verdant dales. In between our route climbs to high moorland, as stark and windswept as the dales are beautiful.

GARRIGILL

After crossing the little bridge over the South Tyne follow the road round to the left. At GR 743421 the road is abandoned for a track on the right. This climbs steeply past Shieldhill to reach the B6277 high on Alston Moor. It offers good views of Garrigill and the vast hillscapes of Cross Fell and its satellites.

The B road is followed to the right for a short while before being left at a sharp bend (GR 751424) for a streamside path (Garrigill Burn), which strikes uphill past the disused Bentyfield Mines. The way-marked path leaves the streamside just before reaching a small plantation of conifers. The way hereabouts is unclear underfoot but if you ignore sheeptracks and follow a

bearing of 45degees ((NE) over the rough grassy moors you should reach the stile in the wall, which lies a couple of hundred yards from the top right-hand corner of the large enclosure. Continue in the same direction across the next field then follow the wall on the right to a stile at a junction of paths (GR 766433). Our route, the right fork, scales the wall and heads for another conifer plantation, whose perimeters are traced (inside the boundary wall).

NENTHEAD

At GR 772436 a way-marking arrow points the way ENE downhill. Below the austere terraced cottages of Nenthead can be seen lining the pallid green valleysides. After passing some ruins by an old grassy track known as Fiddlers Street, the path veers right across more pastures to a lane beyond a five-bar gate. This leads past some houses to reach the Garrigill-Nenthead road at Overwater, a hamlet on the outskirts of Nenthead.

Turn left along the road, then right at the next T-junction and continue past the Crown Inn and over the

The South Tyne runs through a gorge at Garrigill and is easily missed by those with their heads in the air and minds in Allendale.

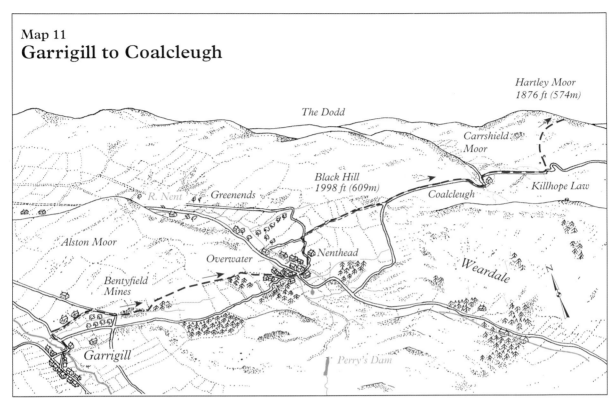

Map 11
Garrigill to Coalcleugh

infant River Nent. After passing the car park you reach the centre of Nenthead village opposite the Miners' Arms.

Nenthead claims to have England's highest house, road and the highest vicarage, church and chapel. This once dog-eared ex-mining village is trying very hard to haul itself into the twentieth century but the mining activities hereabouts have taken more of a toll on the landscape than those of Garrigill and the South Tyne. It boasts a heritage centre, a couple of inns and some nice cottages. Together they put on a much tidier face than in previous years, but at the same time it is still scarred by a huge and ghastly, semi-derelict garage right at its heart and the place is surrounded by unsightly spoil heaps.

Continue across the main road and along a partly cobbled street signposted 'to Greenends'. This climbs to the left and zig-zags past Whitehall Farm. At GR 781441 a stony track to the right climbs to Black Hill. Look back and you should get another glimpse of Cross Fell. In cloudy conditions it really does look dark and menacing, fully deserving its other name, Fiend's Fell.

COALCLEUGH AND THE NORTHUMBERLAND BORDER
A left turn is made along the high road at the summit of Black Hill and a signpost tells us that we are entering Northumberland. In fact this is almost the halfway stage of the walk.

The road descends across bleak moorland to Coalcleugh, another old lead-mining community at the head of the West Allendale, whose pastel green pastures barely separate the wild moorland tops hereabouts.

A right fork 'to Allenheads' is taken beyond Coalcleugh and skirts the empty northern slopes of Killhope Law, a lofty moor (673m) on the Northumberland/Durham border. The road is abandoned just beyond a stream (GR 807455) for a bridleway, ominously titled Black Way and signposted to East Allendale. This is part of an old byway from Teesdale to the Scottish border.

CARRSHIELD MOOR
The route is way-marked with wooden posts and is generally fairly easy to follow. Initially it heads north-

Starting out on the Black Way across Carrshield Moor.

wards, crossing a small stream via a wooden footbridge. It then passes two ruined farmsteads before climbing north-eastwards across the grassy slopes of Carrshield Moor.

HARTLEY MOOR AND KNOCK SHIELD

The shoulder of the moor is traversed and the hollow of the Swinhope Valley appears to the right, leading the eye to the more distant valley of the East Allen and the Coatenhill Reservoir, a small lake which supplied power for the Swinhope Lead Mines. The route, which now rakes across the eastern flanks of Hartley Moor, runs roughly parallel to the Swinhope Valley. It is highlighted by a couple of stone cairns and an H-shaped sheepfold. After fording a stream, ignore the track to the right and maintain the north-easterly direction, descending to a prominent stony track (GR835490), which is followed to its first sharp bend.

More way-marking posts then guide the route across the rough grassy moors to the termination of a country

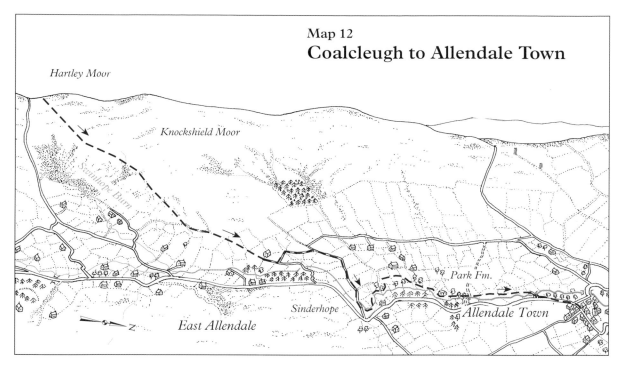

Map 12
Coalcleugh to Allendale Town

lane at GR 838501. This is followed for a short while before turning left at the first junction, passing Knock Shield Farm. A right turn is made at the next junction and the lane is followed down towards the River East Allen.

EAST ALLENDALE

The river is crossed via a one-arched stone bridge. Just beyond it, a left turn is made along a footpath signposted to Holms Linn and Peckriding. It crosses a meadow to the banks of the East Allen and continues delightfully as a grassy path through an avenue of trees. The river is once again crossed via a footbridge to the west bank. Here we see Holms Linn, an attractive waterfall in sylvan surroundings.

The path continues by the riverbanks past a ruined stone-built farmhouse, then enters some woodland close to the huge Holms Farm on the opposite bank. On leaving the woodland it crosses a feeder stream via a small footbridge then climbs westwards over bracken-clad grassy slopes, guided by a line of posts. At a way-marked crossroads of paths a right turn (N) is taken on a lush grassy spur, high above the East Allen, to a wooded dingle. The stile at the edge of this lies furtively by a large pine tree – hidden until the last moment.

Steps lead down to a footbridge over a streamlet and then up the opposite bank.

After continuing parallel to the river and crossing another stream, the path heads for Park Farm (mucky farmyard), which is kept to the left. Ignore the bull signs (which were on the gates marked public footpath) and follow the way-marked path across fields on a course that roughly follows that of the river. Pass by the first footbridge near Studdon park and continue on the riverside path, finally recrossing on the bridge to Peckriding (GR 838544).

NB It is also possible for those with an aversion to road-walking to continue on a more circuitous river and field path east of Woolley Park to meet the road by the bridge at GR 835557. It is a short, sharp climb by road into Allendale Town from here.

ALLENDALE TOWN

The track used by the main route climbs past some cottages to reach the B road half a mile (800m) south of Allendale Town.

The town although not picturesque has great character. It's three and four-storey inns offer clues that this was once a more important town although one, the

The pastures of East Allendale near Allendale Town, looking back south-westwards to the high moors.

Heatherlea Hotel, is due to be converted to an old people's home in 1994.

This place is an ideal night stop with a good deal of accommodation. On our crossing we stayed at the Heatherlea but since its demise we have stopped at the excellent and reasonably priced King's Head. Try their bar meals and if you do stop ask if they have any planned concerts (well sound-proofed in case you are worried about the noise). We watched an excellent folk club on a Friday night; the following week Mike Harding was due to appear.

Allendale Town

Allendale Town is set on a high plinth overlooking a bend in the East Allen River and tucked beneath the heather moors of Hexhamshire Common. On entering the large Market Square with its many large hotels and inns it is obvious that this peaceful place has seen busier times. The town grew with the prosperity of lead and silver mining and at one time had a population of over 5,500, four times the current population. With the death of the industry at the turn of the century agriculture and tourism became more important and at holiday time coach loads of people from the industrial north-east would colonize the village.

One of the England's more colourful ceremonies takes place here – that of the Festival of Fire. Each New Year's Eve at 11.30 pm forty local men, dressed in fancy costumes (guises) and with flaming tar barrels (barls) on their heads, parade around the town streets accompanied by a brass band playing ' Wi' a Hundred Pipes'. Close to midnight they hurl the barrels onto a bonfire and after the church bells chime in the New Year everybody sings ' Auld Lang Syne' before returning to the crowded public houses for more celebrations.

POSSIBLE ALTERNATIVES

You could follow the Alternative Pennine Way from Nenthead to Allendale. It goes over the Dodd, descends Middle Rigg into the West Allen Valley at Ninebanks then climbs Dryburn Moor. From here it descends into Allendale Town via the old chimneys and flue line.

As many of the moors are active grouse moors it is best to keep to the public footpaths

ROUTE FILE	
Distance	13 miles (21 km)
Time	8 hours
Terrain	Good navigational skills required for high grassy and heather-clad moorland, where paths are often obscure underfoot
Escape Routes	None required
Accommodation	Inns and B & Bs in Nenthead. Choice of hotels, inns and B & Bs in Allendale Town
Shops	General store in Nenthead; P.O. in Spartylea; a few shops in Allendale Town

8

ACROSS HEXHAMSHIRE TO THE TYNE VALLEY

Allendale Town to Hexham

This is quite a short section but Hexham is simply too interesting a place to just pass through without exploration.

Lakeland to Lindisfarne climbs out of East Allendale to cross Eshells Moor. The heather-clad expanses of the moor are wide and empty, with only the rising spur of Lambs Rigg and the bracken-clad furrow of Whapweasel Burn breaking the theme.

On descending the moor the route enters a complex of lightly wooded valleys and straddles the high fields between. It passes through the hamlet of Dalton and the earthworks of Dotland's ancient settlement. The charms of the ivy-clad Dipton Mill inn will be hard to resist.

After a pleasant riverside and woodland walk beyond Dipton Mill, we gird our loins for the last short climb of the day over Queen's Letch, wherein lies a story. Now you look across Hexham and the wide valley of the Tyne. In good conditions, the next three days' walk will be laid before your eyes with mile upon mile of undulating Northumbrian uplands stretching to the Cheviot horizon.

Crossing Eshells Moor near Whapweasel Burn.

ALLENDALE TOWN TO HEXHAM
The Main Route

ALLENDALE TOWN
The B6303 Haydon Bridge road is taken out of town and followed on a tight bend around the dene of Philip Burn. A narrow lane to the right then climbs past some charming cottages to high pastures on the eastern side of Allendale. The laneside verges are thickly cloaked with wild flowers in the spring and summer and there are good views back along the dale to the dark moors that are capped by Killhope Law.

MOORHOUSE GATE
Just beyond the farm of Moorhouse Gate, an undulating walled track heads eastwards to a gate at the edge of the vast tract of moorland known as Hexhamshire Common.

ESHELLS MOOR
From the gate, known as Chat's Fell Gate, a rutted track, initially veering slightly left, continues eastward

across the rough grassland of Eshells Moor. The track is intermittent and meanders along a course roughly parallel to a marshy depression on the right.

The grass gradually transforms to a mantle of heather and the track becomes more prominent. The depression on the right deepens to become the course of Whapweasel Burn. Beyond it the swelling spur of Lambs Rigg becomes a further aid to navigation. Views across Hexhamshire Common are now wide and, in late summer, can be colourful with the pinkish purple of the blooming heather interspersed with the greens of the bracken and the darker hues of the pine trees lining the burn.

Eventually the track is joined by a shooters' track climbing out from the opposite side of the burn. The line of the path hereabouts does not exist underfoot. It has been superseded by a shooters' track, which veers left to some grouse butts then right (eastwards) along the line of the butts to rejoin the old track. This is followed through more grassland towards a spruce plantation.

The track terminates at a gate at the edge of farm pastures. Go through the gate and follow the lane to

On the track to Eshells moor near Chat's Fell Gate.

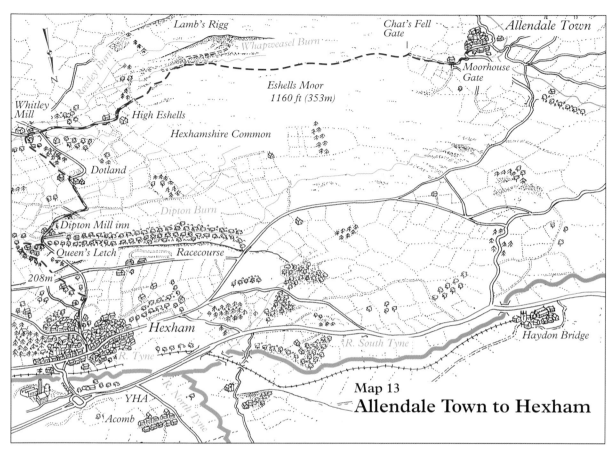

Map 13
Allendale Town to Hexham

High Eshells Farm. When we did our first
Lakeland to Lindisfarne the stream by the
farmhouse had burst its banks and we ended
up avoiding a soaking by clinging to a rickety
old five-bar gate that bridged its course.
Normally there will not be a problem.

DALTON AND WHITLEY MILL
Hedge-lined, seldom-used country lanes lead
past the village of Dalton to the ford at
Whitley Mill (GR 926582).

Do not cross the ford but follow a footpath
at the near side of the footbridge and along-
side the stream, Rowley Burn. It veers to the
left by some woodland to cross a side stream,
Ham Burn, via a footbridge, then climbs
north-westwards up a grassy incline. From
here the course is northwards by a field
divide consisting mainly of a thin line of trees.

The ivy-clad inn at Dipton Mill, an ideal refreshment stop along the way.

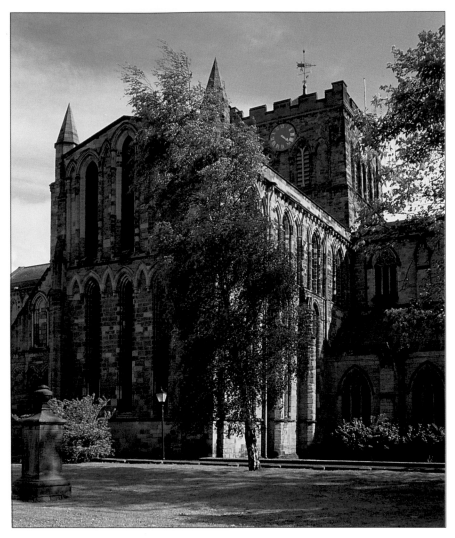

Hexham Abbey, seen above, is one of the finest churches in the North East.

the back. A couple of miles east along the burn is the site of the Battle of Hexham Levels, which took place during the Wars of the Roses. Henry VI and his general, the Duke of Somerset were attacked by the Yorkists who had been waiting in Dipton Wood. Both were captured and the Duke was executed. Henry escaped to Bolton-by-Bowland but was recaptured and executed in London.

Beyond the bridge over Dipton Burn a track to the right leads to a path across fields to the stables of Hole House. At the far side of the house a narrow path squeezes between bushes, climbs down an artificial step to cross a small dyke, then climbs northwards through pleasant woodland.

It continues across high pastures known as Queen's Letch, a place with a story as interesting as its name. During the Wars of the Roses, Queen Margaret was fleeing from the Battle of Hexham Levels with Edward, Prince of Wales when her horse slipped on these slopes. (A letch meant a slip – funny how language changes!) The story continues that they were befriended by a robber from Hexham, who guided them to the safety of what is now known as Queen's Cave (two miles upstream). The robber is said to have fed them until the Yorkists left the area. From here Queen Margaret made her escape, fleeing to France by fishing boat from either Warkworth or Dunstanburgh, depending on which history books you believe.

A track by a ruined building is crossed before reaching the road at the 208 spot height (on 1:50000

DIPTON MILL

After tracing the perimeter of a wooded copse the earthworks of the ancient village of Dotland are passed. A five-bar gate gives entry to the road by Dotland Farm.

If there are no crops in the fields opposite you will be able to follow the footpath northwards to the crossroads at GR 924603 but otherwise continue northwards along the road then right to Dipton Mill. This leafy streamside hamlet has a delightful ivy-clad country inn, which serves lunchtime bar meals in a beer garden at

Hexham

Southern Gateway to the Northumbrian National Park, the abbey town of Hexham basks in the wide valley of the Tyne beneath swelling moorland to the south.

After being given the land by Queen Etheldra of Northumbria, St Wilfred founded his abbey here in AD674. Many of the stones were Roman, probably removed from the fort at nearby Corbridge.

The abbey was to be attacked on many occasions but in 875 Halfdene the Dane ransacked the county and burned the church. Although attempts were made it wasn't until the 1113, when the Augustinians were awarded the land and started the present building, that it was fully restored. The crypt survived the attack and is the finest surviving Saxon structure to be found in Britain. Also surviving St. Wilfred's Chair , 1,300 years old and said to have been the coronation throne of the early Northumbrian Kings.

The abbey survived Henry VIII's dissolution of the monasteries of the 1530s because it was also used as a parish church. The nave and transepts date back to the twelfth and thirteenth century, whilst Dobson's East End and Temple Moore's nave were constructed between 1850 and 1910.

In the shadow of the abbey and also constructed with the help of Roman masonry are the fourteenth-century Moot Hall and Manor Office. The latter, which was the first purpose built gaol in Britain, now houses the tourist information centre and also the fascinating Border History Museum.

In 1761 miners from Allendale, who were objecting to recruitment to the local militia, were read the Riot Act in the Market Square. By the end of the day over 300 were injured and 50 killed. The responsible North Yorkshire Militia were subsequently known as the Hexham Butchers.

Hexham Gaol.

smoke and steam and a brightly coloured 'out of town' superstore are gentle reminders that the densely populated Tyneside area is not that far away.

HEXHAM
When the cottage at the bottom of the fields is neared, a gate in a hedge to the left gives access to the road at GR 935629. The road is then followed for half a mile into Hexham.

maps). If you intend to camp there is a campsite on Hexham Racecourse (National Hunt horse-racing) providing no meeting is being held. There is also a campsite close to the town.

Across the road the path continues northwards. Now the town of Hexham and the verdant Tyne Valley is spread before you with the rolling landscapes of the Northumbrian Uplands and the North Tyne Valley receding to the skyline. An unsightly factory belching

ROUTE FILE	
Distance	10 miles (16 km)
Time	6 hours
Terrain	Begins with rough tracks over heather moors followed by quiet country lanes and footpaths over high pastureland and rolling hillside finally descending to the lowlands of Hexham & the Tyne Valley
Escape Routes	None required
Accommodation	B&B (farmhouse) at Dalton, nr. Whitley Chapel; B&Bs at Juniper Village and Steel just over a mile east of route at Dalton; Many hotels inns & B&Bs at Hexham; youth hostel just over a mile to the north of Hexham at Acomb
Shops	Many shops and stores at Hexham

9

THROUGH THE NORTH TYNE VALLEY

Hexham to West Woodburn

Leaving historical Hexham we enter a land frequented by Roman Legions and once tormented by the violence of battles and treachery. Castles, forts, battlefields and fortified farmhouses all line the route as testament to these turbulent times.

After crossing the River Tyne, Lakeland to Lindisfarne traverses undulating farmland to Acomb and northwards to Hill Head. Here we cross General Wade's seventeenth century military road, built along the line of Hadrian's Wall. This is the site of the Battle of Heavenfield where King Oswald defeated the pagan Cadwalla. Chesters (Roman) Fort is situated just two miles (3km) to the west and is well worth a visit for those with time. Otherwise our route descends to the North Tyne valley at Chollerton and stays roughly parallel to this tributary of the Tyne through the old villages of Barrasford, Gunnerton and Birtley.

After following the riverbanks themselves at Countesspark Wood we enter Redesdale and follow an old track past Iron Age settlements to West Woodburn.

Opposite: The Chesters fort near Chollerford. Below: By the River North Tyne in Countesspark Wood near Redesmouth.

HEXHAM TO WEST WOODBURN
The Main Route

HEXHAM

Hexham is left on the busy northbound road towards the A69 by-pass and the wide, powerfully-flowing waters of the Tyne are crossed. Could this be the river that we first saw on the foothills of Cross Fell?

A tarmac, tree-lined bridleway to the left, preceding the roundabout is then followed. It crosses a bridge over the by-pass and turns right then left along a country lane to reach a five-lane intersection at GR 936656.

ACOMB

All the leafy thoroughfares look inviting but the one to be followed is marked as a cul-de-sac. It leads to the Riding, where a narrow walled track descends into a wooded dene, crosses a bridge over the stream, and climbs out to Acomb, once a coal-mining village. The campsite to the north-east is now built on the reclaimed site of the colliery.

After turning left past eighteenth-century cottages and two pubs take a track to the right (GR 932665). A short stretch near some houses becomes overgrown in the summer months but this can be circumvented by making a parallel course the other side of the hedge in the field to the left (as all the locals have done). The path then heads across fields.

A ladder stile over a wall and hedge marks a change in direction. The stile is scaled and we head north-west-wards for the right-hand corner of the enlarged cottage. Continue in the same direction across a small field to a ladder stile adjacent to the road at Halfway House. Turn right along the lane, which climbs past East Wood. A five-bar gate close to a bend in the road (GR 930682) and just past a line of pylons marks the start of a footpath across fields (which may be planted with cereal crop). Keep to the field boundary then pass through another gate, making for the left (north) corner of a small pine plantation. Do not go though the gate here but follow the fence to the left to reach the country lane at GR 934691. This should be followed to the old Military Road (B6318) at Hill Head, the site of the Battle of Heavenfield AD635. The battle is commemorated by a huge wooden cross (see box). It is also worth noting at this point that Chesters, a superb Roman fort, lies just a mile and a half (2.5km) away at Chollerford. It is well worth seeing if you have the time.

ST OSWALD'S CHAPEL

Hereabouts the road has been built over and along the line of Hadrian's Wall. Take the path by the cross to the old chapel of St Oswald's. A stile at the back of the old graveyard gives access to the footpath which descends grassy banks then heads NNW across the fields, eventually climbing to a ladder stile at the top of a hill. Views from here are wide and interesting. Glimpses of the North Tyne can be seen as it meanders amid verdant rolling countryside. The land is speckled with trees and shrubs and chequered with the occasional field planted with the bright yellow flowers of oil-seed rape. The villages of Chollerton and Humshaugh can plainly be seen. On the horizon you may be able to make out the Scottish border at Carter Bar and the Cheviot and Simonside ridge.

Descending towards Chollerton with the patchwork fields of the North Tyne ahead.

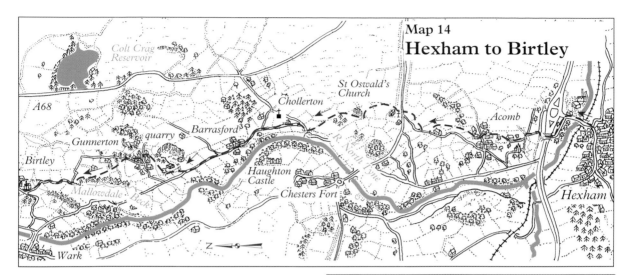

Map 14
Hexham to Birtley

From the hill the line shown on the map will lead you astray – to a barbed wire fence at the edge of some dangerous quarry cliffs. A circuitous path to the right does circumvent the quarries but there is a better route closer to the right of way. After scaling the stile follow a track which descends slightly left between two tall stone gateposts. Narrow, but well-used tracks descend further through bushes and past some derelict winding gear to a small gate. Continue NNW, close to conifer woods with the old fortified tower of Cocklaw Farm prominent to the right. The path meets a country lane at GR 934712 (if in doubt about the exact direction, aim for the one-arched bridge of the disused railway).

CHOLLERTON
Follow the lane under the railway bridge to meet the A6079. A right turn here leads to Chollerton. Chollerton's church is Norman but Roman pillars support the South Arcade. Inside the door is a Roman altar.

BARRASFORD
Beyond the church leave the road for a lane leading to Barrasford, where there is a splendid inn, The Barrasford Arms, serving good meals. (NB The right of way shown following the river is signposted but is overgrown and probably not worth the effort.)

The impressive fourteenth-century Haughton Castle will be noticed, although it is partly enshrouded by trees on the opposite banks of the Tyne. At one time a ferry operated by rope and pulley carried passengers between

King Oswald

Soon after the death of its first Christian king, Edwin, in AD632, Northumbria fell to King Cadwalla of Strathclyde, a barbarous tyrant who ruled with terrible cruelty. Edwin's successors, Eanfrid and Osric were slain in the battle. Oswald, the younger brother of Eanfrid, gathered a small army and marched to meet Cadwalla at Heavenfield. He erected a wooden cross and prayed to God to help him defeat the enemy.

Cadwalla was defeated and killed. It is said to have been the first real victory of Christianity over paganism.

Now Oswald became a good king and tried to spread the word of God by bringing priests to teach his people. One such priest was Aidan. Legend has it that whilst Aidan and Oswald were dining at Bamburgh the servants told them of a group of paupers begging outside for food. The King sent out his own meal and the huge silver dish on which it was served to be shared by the group. Aidan was so impressed that he declared that the King's hand would never perish.

Unfortunately in 642 Oswald was killed in battle near Oswestry by Penda of Mercia. His mutilated body was laid to rest in Bardsley in Lincolnshire. Followers of Oswald brought Oswald's arm back to Bamburgh where it was placed in a silver casket in St Peter's Chapel. Many years later St Bede opened the casket and found the remains still intact.

Traversing moorland on the route two approach to Heugh Farm near Countesspark Woods.

Barrasford and the castle. The agreement for it was entered into during the reign of Henry II.

It is claimed that Haughton Castle was at one time haunted by the bloodcurdling screams of Archie Armstrong, chief of the marauding Border Reivers. He had been thrown into the dungeons by Sir Thomas Swinburne, a seventeenth-century Lord of Haughton, and inadvertently left to starve. The place was exorcised but it is said that if a certain Bible is removed from the castle the haunting will be renewed.

The road is followed from Barrasford to the entrance of the quarries. A hedge-lined track to the left of the entrance is then followed at the edge of the quarry site to a ladder stile.

GUNNERTON

A path keeping a fence to the left then veers north-eastwards to another ladder stile and thence across fields towards some quarry cliffs. Turn left after going through a kissing gate, then follow the line of a wall towards the village of Gunnerton.

A left turn is made through the village, before turning right along another lane. This is followed to GR 901759, a spot recognised by a stone gatepost on a wide, grassy roadside verge. Although the path is non-existent underfoot (at the time of writing), simple stiles or gates are conveniently placed at field boundaries. Turn right following the edge of the field (cereals may be growing in it) to a stile then continue north-westwards over a grassy spur, keeping the Mallowburn woods to the left until GR 892767, level with Pit House. Here the perimeters of the woods should be followed to an intersection of country lanes at the 168m spot height.

BIRTLEY

Take the lane ahead for Birtley. A short-cut path across fields from the bend at GR 883776 can be used to the

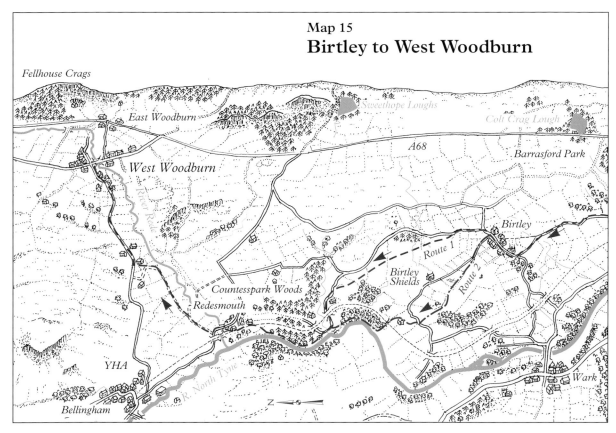

Map 15
Birtley to West Woodburn

village centre, although it can be a little muddy by the stream crossing after heavy rain and a little overgrown with nettles in the latter stages.

Pass through the pleasant village which is largely based on a single street. Those in need of refreshment could make a pit stop at the Percy Arms. There are two alternatives from the village to Countesspark Woods. Route one is a 'summer only' route, otherwise route two is best.

BIRTLEY TO COUNTESSPARK WOODS
ROUTE ONE VIA HIGH CARRY HOUSE
Follow the road out of the village and turn left on a pleasant hedge-lined lane marked 'to Birtley Shields'. At its first corner a way-marked footpath continues straight ahead (westwards) with the field boundary to the right. The fence is crossed near some woods via a ladder stile and the path (trackless) heads north-westwards across fields past a ruined farmhouse north of High Carry House. Above the ruins a stile leads to the

next field and the path turns right (NE) by the fence along a field full of thistles. There are extensive views of the North Tyne valley and back to the high Pennines, including Cross Fell.

After crossing a dyke the path descends to cross the old North Tyne Railway at a cutting. Two stiles mark the entry and exit. (A local farmer told me that the railway was being used as a footpath all the way to Redesmouth but there is no right of access and landowners have every right to turn you back.)

Now head northwards across a field, descending towards the riverbanks. A primitive stile by a large tree in the right hand corner of the field marks the entry to the woods and a steep, slippery path leads down to the water's edge. This would be interesting, to say the least, after rain or outside the summer months. A rough path now weaves though the woodland to reach a field that is sometimes used for equestrian events. Continue parallel to the river and through the ruins of an old enclosure to cross a footbridge over a dyke. The route meets route two at the gate in the forest ahead. (For the continuation of the route see Countesspark Woods.)

BIRTLEY TO COUNTESSPARK WOODS
ROUTE TWO VIA HEUGH FARM
Continue along the lane out of Birtley, taking the left fork at GR 881785 to the bend at GR 878790. Here a simple step stile on the left gives access to the unmarked and 'invisible on the ground' footpath. This heads north-westwards across rough pastures, crosses a small stream, Holywell Burn, and goes through a gate about halfway between two woods (the one on the left is marked on the map with a homestead.)

The path gradually veers NNW between the woods. There are wooden gates at the relevant field boundaries. Another larger mixed plantation appears to the left. The line of the path is roughly parallel to this, with the farmhouse of Heugh and the riverside plantations of Countesspark Wood directly ahead. Another high farm, Buteland, appears, dramatically perched on a hilltop to their right.

A rutted track develops and this leads to a lane west of Heugh. The winding lane descends past the farm and under the old railway bridge to the conifer plantations of High Countess Park. In the woods above Heugh Burn are the earthwork remains of an early British settlement.

At a sharp bend by a stone-built cottage (GR 869805) the lane is abandoned and we descend grassy meadows towards the banks of the North Tyne. A gate marks the start of the path through the mixed woodlands of Countesspark Woods where we meet route one.

COUNTESSPARK WOODS AND REDESMOUTH
Initially the narrow path beyond the gate can be muddy but it soon develops into a pleasant cart track following the course of the wide river. The cart track ends at a turning circle and another narrow path continues, climbing to a stile at the northern edge of the plantation.

Beyond it we turn left, following the line of a dismantled railway. The platform of the old Redesmouth station is still intact. Just beyond it the path continues to a small gate by some cottages. Follow the lane and make a right turn to reach the Bellingham Road.

This tree-lined lane is followed to the left over the River Rede, close to its confluence with the North Tyne. The abutments of the old railway bridge still

stand adjacent to the road bridge. A short way up the lane, near a sharp bend (GR 859826), our route continues on a track signposted 'The Border County Ride'. This green road winds through cow pastures for half a mile (800km) before being left for a less-defined track to the left (beyond a five-bar gate). The new track climbs over more reedy terrain close to the earthworks of an old settlement near the 159 spot height and continues to an old stone barn (GR 869843), where it turns sharp left.

This grassy track is abandoned as it turns left, back towards Rawfoot Farm. Our route (way-marked) goes straight on, fording a tree-enshrouded burn before climbing along the field edge, passing to the left of Hole Farm, which has an adjacent bastle.

We now have to use the lane for nearly three miles (5km) to West Woodburn but at least it is quick. You could detour on the path from the east of Low Leam but it is quite rough and, frankly, not worth the effort. Maybe its time for a spot of running? Well, perhaps not.

WEST WOODBURN
The village has two inns for those who want to take their well-earned rest. The Bay Horse has just been refurbished and looks very pleasant.

Close by, in the middle of the riverside fields, are the earthworks of Habitancvm. This was an important Roman outpost fort in the third century for cavalrymen known as the Exploratores Habitancensis. It was the first outpost on Dere Street for northbound soldiers from Corbridge. It can best be viewed from the metalled farm track, which heads south westwards to The Cragg (farm) from the main road at GR 894867.

ROUTE FILE

Distance	19 miles (30 km)
Time	10 hours
Terrain	Varied. Paths across pastures and cereal fields; country lanes
Accommodation	Inn, B&Bs and Youth Hostel at Acomb; Barrasford Arms and B&Bs at Barrasford; youth hostel and campsite at Bellingham (1mile off route from Redesmouth); 2 Inns and B&Bs at West Woodburn
Shops	P. O./general stores at Barrasford, Gunnerton, Birtley and West Woodburn

10

OVER THE SIMONSIDE HILLS

West Woodburn to Rothbury

From the sombre fields of Redesdale to the picturesque and verdant valley of Coquetdale, Lakeland to Lindisfarne displays the rich diversity of its landscapes.

On leaving West Woodburn it climbs the afforested craggy slopes of Raylees Common then descends to Elsdon, a typical Northumbrian border village with a bastle, large green and the remains of an old castle. From here a winding country lane leads to Harwood Forest, where a fast pace is set through legions of pine and spruce.

For those who wish to stick with the mountains for as long as possible I have offered a Cheviot Loop (*see*

Chapter 14). This diverts at Fallowlees in the Harwood Forest and straddles the heather moors of Boddle Moss to the south of Tosson Hill.

The main route heads for Simonside, the most popular peak of the Simonside Hills. This superb craggy ridge overlooking Coquetdale is covered with a mantle of heather – it's a joy to walk and easy too. If conditions are clear walkers will get their first views of the North Sea.

Beyond the ridge, the route visits the ancient high fort of Lordenshaws before descending to Rothbury, one of the prettiest villages in the county.

Looking westwards to Dove Crag and Simonside from the most easterly unnamed summit.

WEST WOODBURN TO ROTHBURY
The Main Route

WEST WOODBURN

From West Woodburn we follow the winding lane towards Town Head past some cottages. At GR 898872 a signposted footpath begins on steps over the dry-stone wall and continues NNE across fields, descending to a stone bridge that is used to cross the River Rede. Turn left beyond the bridge on a riverside footpath through woodland. This can be muddy after rain.

The track is abandoned after crossing a footbridge over a feeder stream. A right of way, unclear underfoot, climbs northwards above the woodland. It then veers north-eastwards across bracken-clad slopes to reach a country lane (GR 902883) beneath the spruce forests that cloak Raylees Common.

A right turn is made along the lane to a way-marked footpath which then climbs north-eastwards on grassy rides through the forests and over the scrubby boulder slopes of Fellhouse Crags.

WETHER HILL

Above Fellhouse Crags the continuation of the path is slightly to the right of the obvious rutted track and straddles the dry-stone wall by way of some steps (highlighted in whitewash at present). It descends slightly from here along another grassy ride before climbing to the open fellsides. Here the plantation's edge is traced to the trig point on the summit of Wether Hill.

RAYLEES

A stone wall to the right guides the way down grassy flanks. The wall is eventually crossed via a ladder stile and the path heads for the cluster of cottages that form the hamlet of Raylees.

Nearing the road, the path passes to the left of a cottage with the well-preserved earthworks of a moat. After crossing the busy A696 continue straight ahead on the narrow lane climbing the hillsides beyond. On

On the village green at Elsdon with the church on the right and the pele tower overlooking the back of the green.

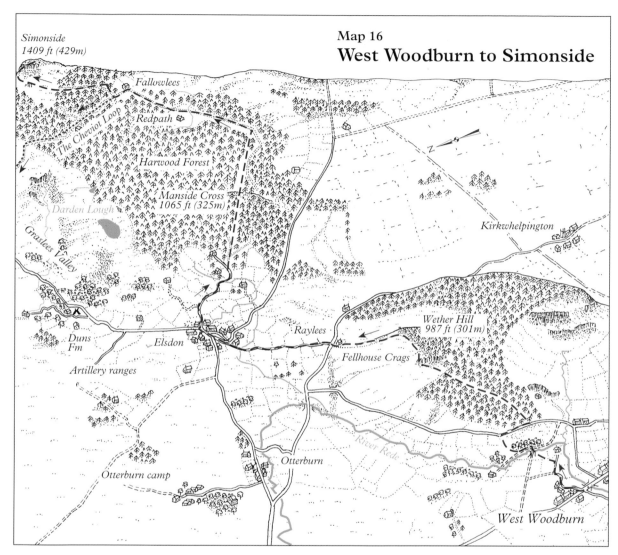

Map 16
West Woodburn to Simonside

reaching the summit of the lane, there is a good panorama. The village of Elsdon lies in a wide verdant bowl beneath afforested hills which are capped by the shapely sandstone escarpments of the Simonside Hills. To the north the beautiful Grasslees Valley is dappled with the colours of bracken, heather and woodland – a glorious site in autumn.

ELSDON

The road now descends into Elsdon. This historic village, once considered the capital of Redesdale, is well worth exploring. Eighteenth - and nineteenth-century stone cottages surround the large village greens, which are separated by the church and graveyard. Many of the dead from the Battle of Otterburn were buried in the graveyard. Elsdon Tower, built around 1400 and still occupied, is a fine example of a pele tower. At one time Elsdon was situated on the line of an old drove road from Newcastle to Scotland and would have been subject to frequent raids from the infamous Border Reivers.

To the north of the village are the earthworks that remain from the Norman motte and bailey castle. Built by the Umfavilles soon after the Conquest, the castle

Selby's Cove, seen on the trek across the heather moor between the Harwood Forest and the Simonside Ridge.
Crags on Simonside with Rothbury and the Coquet Valley below.

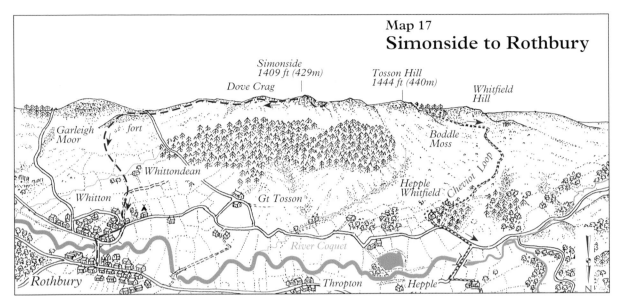

Map 17
Simonside to Rothbury

was occupied until the mid-twelfth century when it was abandoned for Harbottle Castle, just eight miles to the north-east.

From the eastern side of Elsdon's village green a gated road, marked 'to East Nook' is followed. It climbs through farm pastures to the extensive conifer plantations of the Harwood Forest. At Whitelees Farm a signposted footpath climbs though pine trees to meet a forest track at a junction (GR 963926).

HARWOOD FOREST AND MANSIDE CROSS

Still signposted, the path continues on a rough grassy forest ride (fire break) climbing steadily eastwards to Manside Cross. On the highest gound there there are some earthworks, remains of an ancient fort and also the stone plinth of an old cross. It is quite possible that you will spy a roe deer in this locality – I saw two or three of the timid creatures on my first visit.

FALLOWLEES

From Manside Cross the path descends by a fence at the edge of a narrow swathe of rough grassland, briefly encountering a forest track at GR 993920. At GR 001918 another forest track is followed to the left (north-eastwards past Redpath Farm). The footpath shown from here is overgrown at present and it is better to keep on the forestry road to Fallowlees, where it turns left. Turn right at the next crossroads unless you want to do the Cheviot Loop (you will go straight on,

following the bridleway sign for Chartners – *see* Chapter 14).

The track used by the main route descend northwards to cross Newbiggin Burn and past a large disused quarry. It is abandoned at a sharp right-hand bend (GR 022963). Here a firm grassy ride leads to a stile at the edge of the forest.

There is a feeling of exhilaration and freedom on setting foot across the open heather moorland that lies ahead. On the skyline are the craggy outlines of the Simonside Hills. The exact line of the path marked on the map is non-existent underfoot. There is, however, a narrow track, which heads north-westwards to the edge of the forest, which it then traces north-eastwards (the best bet if the weather is dodgy). Alternatively you can strike ahead, aiming for the crags (Selby's Cove) seen in the mid-distance preceding the main ridge.

SELBY'S COVE

The steel-grey faulted cliffs of Selby's Cove rear up from a boulder-strewn plinth of heather and bracken. Not surprisingly it is a popular place with climbers. The path is shown as re-entering the forest hereabouts but the better course is to use the well-defined path along its perimeter.

SIMONSIDE

It continues beneath the western flanks of Simonside before tackling the hill on a steep path between crags to

Rothbury, one of Northumberland's prettiest villages.

the summit cairn. Views from the top are spectacular. Below is Coquetdale. The river meanders lazily amidst emerald plains, while the villages of Thropton and Rothbury bask beneath forest-clad, craggy hills. Further afield the attention is grabbed by the Cheviots. Smaller, more shapely foothills surround the big flat-topped Cheviot like servants at court. To the east the heather-cloaked Simonside ridge leads the eye to the coast, which can be traced from Tyneside to the Tweed.

DOVE CRAG

A good path continues eastwards along the ridge, bypassing Simonside's east summit to the north on a direct route to Dove Crag. Here clifftop views over Rothbury are more intimate than those of Simonside. The church's square tower can now be seen standing proud of the clustered rooftops.

The narrow path continues to a third unnamed peak (360m spot height), whose heather-clad top is crowned by a stone shelter. Views north-eastwards towards the lower eminences of Garleigh Moor reveal the shadowy lines of Lordenshaws, a bronze age Romano-British hillfort.

GARLEIGH MOOR AND LORDENSHAWS

We now descend to a laneside car park at GR 052988. The gateposts at the back of the car park mark the commencement of a confusing system of paths and grassy tracks. It is best to follow the rutted track (a new 'pre-

ferred' concessionary route and not the right of way) heading for the fort on the top of the hill. On reaching the fort the track degenerates into sheep-tracks. Descend north-eastwards on a heathery spur, a line roughly parallel with the depression beneath the craggy hill to the east.

A stile across a fence traversing Garleigh Moor marks the recommencement of way-marking. From here a descent is made northwards towards Rothbury, which has reappeared in the valley below.

White wood posts mark the downhill path across fields. The stream in WhittonDean is forded and the path climbs out to cross another field to reach an enclosed farm track (GR 057006), known as Hillhead Road. Turn right along the track past the tower of Sharpe's Folly to a country lane in the hamlet of Whitton.

ROTHBURY

A left turn is made along the lane before leaving it for a signposted footpath which doubles back (NE) on high, sloping fields to descend to the outskirts of Rothbury. It joins a metalled lane descending to the road bridge across the River Coquet, which hereabouts is wide but still lively. The picturesque, self-acclaimed Capital of Coquetdale lies just the other side. Stone cottages, shops and inns surround an expansive tree-lined green. This is one of the most pleasant places on the whole route – do not pass it by too quickly!

ROUTE FILE

Distance	18 miles (29 km)
Time	10 hours
Terrain	Country lanes and forest tracks followed by firm ridge walks on the Simonside Fells
Accommodation	Hotels, inns, B&Bs and campsite at Rothbury. Campsite at Dunns Farm off route 3 miles north of Elsdon
Shops	Quite a few shops in Rothbury

11

FROM COQUETDALE TO ALNWICK

Rothbury to Alnwick

From Rothbury we leave the hills and go for the coast. There is no quick way for much of the land is private with few useful footpaths. Lakeland to Lindisfarne *does* find a good way though – it just meanders a little.

First it weaves through pleasant scenery on the southern banks of the River Coquet to Pauperhaugh Bridge. Craggy, wooded hills form a backdrop on both flanks.

We then discover a 'green' road along Framlington Common before descending into an idyllic valley where lies the hamlet of Edlingham. Here in the midst of peaceful pasture are the ruins of an old castle, an impressive viaduct and a charming little church.

The route then scales Alnwick Moor, its very last hill. From this heather-cloaked hill with fine views over fell and coast, we descend upon Alnwick's medieval fortress town – maybe the marauding Scots would have come this way in times past.

Alnwick is the grandest town encountered along the route – a heady mix of history and legend.

The Coquet Valley from the old railway line above Wagtail Farm, Rothbury.

ROTHBURY TO ALNWICK
The Main Route

ROTHBURY

The road bridge over the River Coquet is crossed and a left turn is made along the Hexham Road. This is soon quitted for Mill Lane, a narrow metalled cul-de-sac on the left-hand side. The lane turns into a track and we leave Rothbury behind. It assumes a course parallel to but high above the meandering southern banks of the Coquet. To the north are the sprawling woodlands of Cragside. Victorian entrepreneur Sir William Armstrong built his thousand acre country estate here, on the edge of rough moorland. It consists of a huge stone and timber mansion surrounded by woodland. The place is especially resplendent in June when the rhododendrons and azaleas are in bloom.

WAGTAIL FARM

The right of way shown on the maps as veering left off the track towards the river is overgrown and virtually unusable. Our route (a permissive path) continues on the track beyond Wagtail Farm. We are now on the for-mer course of a railway. It enters pleasant woodland and carves a deep cutting through crags.

Keep an eye out for a step stile by a gate (left) beyond the cutting. Here the path leaves the old railway and continues eastwards across a field towards an old cottage. A farm track is now followed over fields to West Row where it turns right. Turn left at a crossroads of tracks, a short way beyond the farmhouse and follow the line of the hedge to the left.

On reaching a small cottage, a left turn is made through a gate and over a stile. Now take the second gate on the right and follow the hedge parallel to a little valley to the right. A wooden gate allows a brief entry into the woods before emerging in another field with a dyke immediately to the right. The dyke is followed to a little bridge over it, which is crossed.

PAUPERHAUGH BRIDGE

The footpath now heads for the banks of the Coquet, which are followed to the fine, three-arched, stone-built Pauperhaugh Bridge.

Cross the bridge to the junction with the B road. Turn right, passing Priors Gate and first left along the lane to a sharp corner (GR 108000). Now follow the

The River Coquet from Pauperhaugh Bridge.

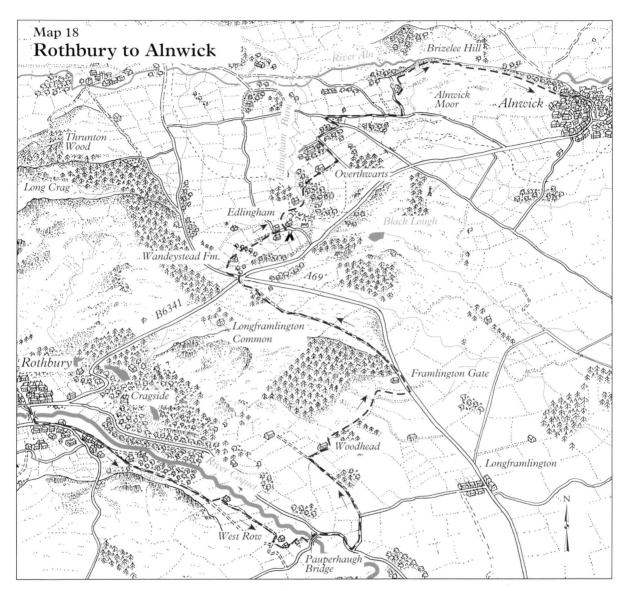

Map 18
Rothbury to Alnwick

farm lane northwards to a junction with the drive of Woodhead Farm. After passing to the right of the farm follow the fence beyond it to a five-bar gate. Go through the gate then diagonally across a field and through a gap in the top wall, keeping the conifer plantation well to the right. Follow the wall over reedy fields past the north-western perimeter of the previously mentioned plantation.

After passing the top edge of a second plantation the bridleway climbs away from the high fields to the edge

of the open moorland of Mount Pleasant (not named on 1:50000 maps).

LONGFRAMLINGTON COMMON
Although still legal the bridleway becomes overplanted and impassable in the huge spruce woods on Longframlington Common. It is thus more prudent to turn right along the bridleway to the Wooler Road (GR 121030). After following the road briefly northwards to Framlington Gate, a gravelly track to the left takes us

Crossing the moors on the bridleway across Longframlington Common.
The castle at Edlingham, a tiny hamlet in a secluded rural valley.

back to the moors, skirting the edge of the forest before traversing Long-framlington Common. There are new views across wide open spaces to the bold outlines of the Cheviot Hills.

The track meets the Rothbury to Alnwick road near the crossroads with the busy A697. (There is a B&B at New Moor House on the crossroads at present.)

Turn left along the A697 before leaving it for a signposted and way-marked path. This heads northwards across fields to Wandeystead Farm, fording a stream *en route*. After passing through the farmyard

The Edlingham Valley from Corby Crags. The castle and viaduct are visible in the mid-distance.

the path continues, climbing northwards along a rutted track. This is abandoned halfway along the first field. The way, which is unclear underfoot, is half right to the top right corner of the field, then round the back of the grassy knoll by a fence. Go through a gate in the fence (marked by a yellow arrow), then immediately right, though an adjacent gate.

EDLINGHAM

A bearing of about 20 degrees across the field should lead you to the next gate two-thirds of the way along its tree-lined top edge (Long Plantation). From here we are guided by a fence to the right to a farm track (very mucky when I used it) passing Demesne Farm.

A lane now descends into Edlingham, one of the most pleasantly sited hamlets in Northumberland. Beautifully tucked away beneath heather-clad, craggy hills, it is surrounded by verdant pastures etched by the ridge and furrow of the medieval plough. There are ruins of a thirteenth-century castle, an elaborate tower house, an impressive stone railway viaduct and a Norman church.

A path signposted 'Lemmington Hall' begins at a gate to the left of the church entrance. It then goes right (north-east) across fields past the castle and over the disused railway, well to the left of the viaduct. Continue

by the fence, descending towards a wooded dene. After about 300yd (275m) (halfway to the trees) leave the fence and head northwards down to a gate at the edge of the woods.

Edlingham Burn is crossed via a footbridge and the path climbs to the opposite edge and uphill to Overthwarts farm. Continue along the farm track to the road.

Turn left along the lane, passing the beautiful woods of Lemmington Hall, then left at a T-junction on the 73m spot height. Turn right shortly after and follow the lane climbing away from the cultivated landscapes of pasture and woodland to the wilder environs of Broome Hill. The rough hills on both sides are part of Alnwick Moor.

ALNWICK MOOR

A left turn is made along the lane at GR 146127, passing an area of marshland frequented by a myriad gulls. The lane to be used is at present marked with the military signs for Brizelee Wood, a radar station which has now been dismantled. Watch out for a ladder stile over the stone wall to the right. Scale it and climb north-eastwards across the heather moors to reach the tall stone wall, which is followed downhill towards Alnwick. The other side of the wall is Hulne Park, private gardens

About Alnwick

Lying as it did so close to Scotland at the lowest bridging point of the Aln, Alnwick was the scene of many a fierce battle and was therefore a natural place for a castle.

The origins of Alnwick Castle date back to the eleventh century when it was constructed for Norman baron Yvo de Vesey to control the Great North Road. It was bought by Henry de Percy in 1309 along with the title, First Earl of Northumberland. The family emblem, a lion with a rigid tail, is often seen and stands sentry over the town on the top of a huge column, built in 1816.

In the fourteenth century the castle was enlarged and created an invincible fortress. Battles with the Scots, particularly the Douglas family, are well documented. Harry Hotspur, the most famous of Percys, plays a large roll in Shakespeare's Henry V and is seen as a bloodthirsty man with a lust for spilling Scottish blood. Unfortunately, in those early days, the unprotected townspeople didn't fare quite so well with the Scots and were frequently raided. In the fifteenth century, however, town walls were added.

On the union with Scotland the troubles subsided and the walls were dismantled, leaving only the impressive stone-built tower gates for us to view today.

About this time, the Percys moved south leaving Alnwick Castle itself to fall derelict. The male line of the family was terminated in 1670 with the death in Turin of the eleventh Earl. Many years later his great-granddaughter married a Yorkshireman, Sir Hugh Smithson. In 1750 Sir Hugh changed his name to Percy and in 1766 became the first Duke of Northumberland. He had the castle fully restored by James Payne and Robert Adam. Later the interior was transformed again in Italian Renaissance style by Anthony Salvin; works by Titian, Van Dyke and Canoletto hang on the walls.

The Dukes' gardens now known as Hulne Park were added, designed by Capability Brown. In their grounds are the remains of a priory and abbey and also a 90ft folly, the Brizelee Tower. It is said that from it you can spy over seven castles, probably Chillingham, Warkworth, Dunstanburgh, Bamburgh, Lindisfarne, Ross and Alnwick.

Below and opposite: Alnwick Castle.

belonging to the Duke of Northumberland. They were designed by Capability Brown and can be visited on Saturdays and Sundays. It is a pity you cannot visit them now for that big wall seems to lock you out; did it have to be so high?

ALNWICK
On the descent the terrain changes from heathland to marshy scrubland and then to pastureland in the lower reaches.

Beyond a stream crossing tracks head for the outskirts of the town through urban commons, emerging by the Forest Lodge and ornamental gates of Hulne Park. Just beyond the lodge is a stone commemorating the capture in 1172 of William the Lion, King of Scotland.

Continue along Ratten Row, which leads into Bailiffgate, a pleasing tree-lined street with buildings of sandstone. Here the cavalry from the castle would have exercised. The castle can be seen at the end of the street. If you are in no hurry and want to get a good view of it, turn left down the Peth and follow the riverbanks for a hundred yards (90m).

To get to the town centre, turn right by the castle walls and go along Narrowgate, an interesting curved street with some fine old buildings.

Being a major stop-off on the Great North Road, Alnwick has many old coaching houses, including the Black Swan and the Old Cross Inn, both on Narrowgate. The Old Cross Inn is known locally as Dirty Bottles. About 160 years ago the innkeeper died when dressing the window with bottles. His widow refused to let the bottles be removed and it is said that if anybody tries to move or disturb them they will meet with an untimely death. Needless to say the dusty bottles lie untouched in the window to this day.

Narrowgate leads into Bondgate and the town centre shops and hotels. If you want the tourist information centre, turn right along Market Street, where a line of tall trees divides the modern road and an old street of cobbles. The centre is in Northumberland Hall, the impressive cloistered building by the Market Square.

POSSIBLE ALTERNATIVES

From Edlingham it is possible to climb the heather hills eastwards on the bridleway south of Black Lough, though it is rough and trackless in places. Farm lanes would then lead north past Freemans Hill to the country lanes south of Alnwick. Many of the footpaths in this area are unsignposted and difficult to find without the aid of an OS Pathfinder map.

Another alternative would be to link the riverside paths of the Coquet Valley, past Brinkburn and Felton to Warkworth, a fine castle town. A seaside route could then be continued northwards, coming inland temporarily to round the Aln estuary at Alnmouth. Unfortunately, on this route, Alnwick would be missed.

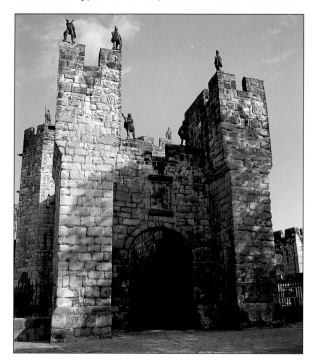

ROUTE FILE	
Distance	18 miles (29 km)
Time	9 hours
Terrain	Varied. Paths across pastures tracks across both heather and grassy moorland; country lanes
Accommodation	Campsite (late May and summer) at Edlingham; Inns, hotels & B&Bs in Alnwick
Shops	Many shops and stores at Alnwick. Market day is Saturday and early closing is on Wednesday

12

TO THE COAST

Alnwick to Beadnell

At the end of this day you will have completed a coast-to-coast if not the whole walk and there will be a tinge of success as you dip your toes in the North Sea.

From Alnwick's proud castle the route meanders along riverbanks of the Aln to the picturesque little village of Lesbury, then finally to the coast near Boulmer.

The fresh air of the seaside is exhilarating at any time but especially bracing after nearly 150 miles of hillwalking. It will probably stir a few memories for those who traded their bucket and spades for crampons and heavy boots. Suddenly the urge to hurry has gone. I found myself having to be dragged away from the rock pools where I searched for crabs and starfish. The villages, such as Craster, Newton and Boulmer are not as picturesque as their Cornwall counterparts but have a rustic charm of their own.

The rugged coastline transforms many times from craggy coves to wide-sweeping bays with sand-dunes and heughs (small hills).

The ruins of Dunstanburgh Castle, set on dark dramatic cliffs north of Craster, are probably the most spectacular sight of the day but those last two miles along the wide beaches from Newton Links to Beadnell Harbour may be the most satisfying.

Opposite: The River Aln near Bilton Mill between Alnwick and the coast. Below: Approaching the Bathing House near Howick.

ALNWICK TO BEADNELL
The Main Route

ALNWICK

From south of the Bondgate Tower take the Bamburgh B road by the tall Tenantry Column. After a short distance turn right along a pedestrianized lane by a new housing estate (GR193132). The lane becomes an unsurfaced cart track and heads eastwards. At its termination a footpath continues in the same direction across fields. The buzz of traffic can be heard from the busy A1 highway. The path meets another cart track and this in turn leads to a surfaced lane which heads south-westwards to the A1068 Alnmouth road. The road is followed over the A1 to Alndyke. The River Aln can now be seen meandering amidst barley-decked fields parcelled by hedgerow and woodland.

A signposted footpath beyond the house traverses fields, descending to the banks of the Aln. The waters of this river, fringed with reeds and lined with trees, are still, sullen and deep. The path traces its southern banks.

After crossing a feeder stream via a footbridge the path meets a lane south of a deep river ford. Turn right along the lane for a few yards then left on a track which rounds Bilton Mill, then continues by the river. Beyond a conifer plantation the track degenerates into a river-side footpath, which is followed on a winding course beneath the huge viaduct (built 1846) of the Kings Cross to Edinburgh railway.

LESBURY

The river wriggles southwards and the footpath duly follows it, entering a narrow strip of woodland before climbing out once more to the field's edge. It emerges at a stone bridge conveying the busy Alnmouth-Alnwick road through the village of Lesbury. Cross the bridge and turn right into the village centre.

The street is lined with attractive cottages and an interesting church, with origins in the thirteenth century. There is a well-stocked post office/general store and also a good inn for those in need of sustenance.

At the far end of the village along the Longhoughton road, a footpath sign between two cottages points the way across fields and down to the riverside. Once again you will probably be walking at the edge of cereal-cropped fields but the path is a good one. At GR 245118 a junction of paths is shown on the map and the stiles and gates for both exist. We want the upper one but outside the winter months this will necessitate walking through crops. It is more prudent to use the lower one to the last of the planted fields then follow the fence upwards to the stile where the upper path continues ESE to the road at GR 250116. We are now in an elevated position and retrospective views are good. The River Aln meanders like a serpent through flat pastures, chequered with green and oatmeal. Lesbury and Hipsburn nestle in undulating countryside decked with field and wood, and parcelled by winding lanes.

FOXTON HALL

On crossing the road, follow the metalled lane immediately opposite to Foxton Hall, now the clubhouse for the local golf club. A narrow path then sneaks through a natural wooded ginnel and finally to the seashore. Last one to the water's a sissy!

Cottages at Lesbury, the last village before the coast.

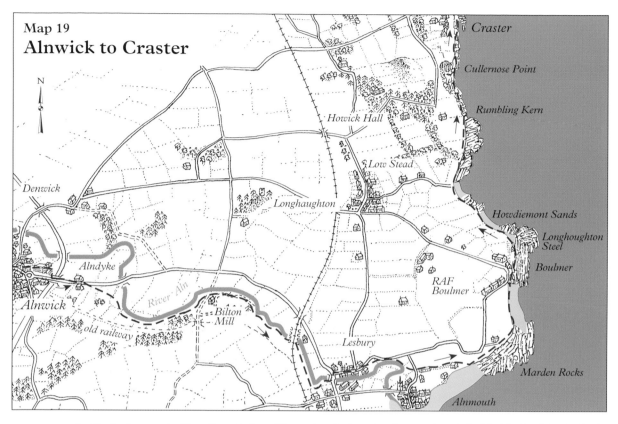

Map 19
Alnwick to Craster

N

Craster
Cullernose Point
Rumbling Kern
Howick Hall
Low Stead
Howdiemont Sands
Longhoughton Steel
Boulmer
Denwick
Longhaughton
RAF Boulmer
Alndyke
River Aln
Bilton Mill
Alnwick
old railway
Lesbury
Marden Rocks
Alnmouth

Looking back across the River Aln to Lesbury. The patchwork of cereal and pasture is typical of the Northumbrian lowlands.

The harbour at Craster. This pleasant Northumberland fishing village is famous for its kippers.

ON THE COAST

The salt water and sand mingles with the toes to refresh and rejuvenate sore feet. But although we have done a coast-to-coast, there are a few miles to go yet; this Gillham's a hard task-master!

Continuing along the shore there's a great feeling of achievement and optimism for the journey still to come. Out to sea is Coquet Island, a rocky knoll with a light-house and an ancient Benedictine Cell which was once home to St Cuthbert.

The coastal paths are all self-evident. At this stage I should point out that, in Britain, it is legal to walk the beaches on land lying between the low and high water marks. More often than not it will be possible to walk along the beach – and it is always more pleasant to do so. The firmer, more comfortable sand (i.e. the stuff that doesn't sift through your boots and socks at every opportunity) lies closest to the waves.

If the tide is low, it is best to walk along the shore, whose sands are punctuated by craggy reefs, rock pools and seaweed. Always be watchful of the tide and divert to the inner footpaths if it comes in!

Our route heads northwards along the shores and around Seaton Point where the gritstone slabs known as Marden Rocks jut out to the sea. You may see some brittle-stars, a type of starfish.

BOULMER

The gritstone at Seaton Point is accompanied by the harder dolerite as Boulmer is approached. The village's natural harbour, Boulmer Haven, is almost protected by the rocks which cradle the sandy beach. On the shores you may spot the shells of periwinkles, limpets and razor-shells.

Boulmer's rustic stone cottages line a street which comes very close to the seashore The little village and its inn, The Fishing Boat, have traditions of smuggling and it wasn't unusual for barrels of liquor to be found hidden beneath the sands. An RNLI lifeboat once sailed from here but the rescue service is now

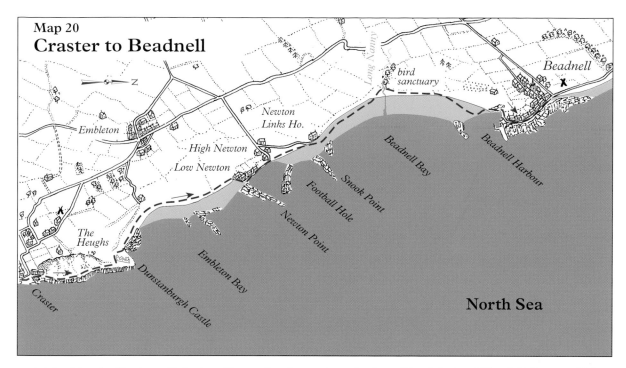

Map 20
Craster to Beadnell

Embleton

Newton Links Ho.

High Newton

Low Newton

Newton Point

Football Hole

Snook Point

Beadnell Bay

bird sanctuary

Long Nanny

Beadnell

Beadnell Harbour

The Heughs

Embleton Bay

Dunstanburgh Castle

Craster

North Sea

maintained by the Boulmer Volunteer Rescue Service, using the old lifeboat station. RAF Boulmer operates rescue helicopters.

The path continues along the rocks (or on the fields above them if the tide is high) and around Longhoughton Steel to Howdiemont Sands. Here there is a road terminus.

Further north a footbridge is used to cross the outlet of a stream which has meandered through the wooded dene of Howick Burn. From here you can continue along the shoreline or follow a path slightly inland. Keep well away from the badly eroded sandstone cliffs. Primroses and cowslips number amongst the colourful flora seen along this higher route. The rocks known as Rumbling Kern contain a large hole through which the sea surges.

HOWICK HALL

At Howick Haven, a short way north of Rumbling Kern, the shore is left. A path climbs towards the Bathing House, built for the wealthy Grey family from nearby Howick Hall. Harsh elements have eaten well into the masonry of this Victorian dwelling, below which is a rectangular bathing pool. The path continues along the clifftop. North of Howick it is confined by

thorn bushes. The dolerite cliffs of Cullernose Point, which jut out to sea, are colonized by fulmars and the whole place can be filled with their plaintive cries.

CRASTER

From the Point the route continues across wide coastal pastures into Craster, a small fishing village renowned for its kippers (they have their own secret recipe). Cobles still fish for lobsters and herring, but much of the stock for the factories is now imported.

If you started the day in Alnwick by the time you reach Craster it will probably be about lunchtime. In the centre of the village there is a good pub serving reasonably priced snacks and there is also a licensed café.

DUNSTANBURGH CASTLE

After rounding the harbour our route continues on the seafront across grassland to the east of the Heughs (low hills). Ahead are the impressive ruins of Dunstanburgh Castle. On reaching it we find that the castle is perched on high whin sill cliffs above Queen Margaret's Cove. (Queen Margaret is the same lady whose horse slipped at Queen's Letch south of Hexham; she possibly escaped to France from here – Warkworth claims that

she escaped from there.) The castle's construction was instigated by Thomas, Earl of Lancaster, in 1313. It was once home to the Earl of Northumberland's great friend, John of Gaunt, and briefly became a royal castle when John of Gaunt's son became Henry IV. It was attacked by the Scots and also besieged by the Yorkists during the Wars of the Roses.

EMBLETON BAY

A charge is made for visiting the castle. Our route by-

passes it to the left before descending away from the golf course and tall sand dunes to the wide curving beach at Embleton Bay. This stretch is a glorious one. The strange twisted rock strata of Saddle Rock rises proud of the beach and always the silhouette of Dunstanburgh Castle dominates subtly changing retrospective views.

At high tide, and after periods of heavy rain, it may be necessary to head inland to use the footbridge at the Snaith – otherwise the walk is unbroken to the bay of

Left: Looking along the rocky shoreline at Craster towards the impressive ruins of Dunstanburgh Castle. This was once a Royal castle, home to Henry V, son of John of Gaunt. Above: Enjoying a cup of tea at the Ship Inn in Low Newton-by-the-Sea on a crisp winter day.

Newton Haven. Often you will see wind surfers riding the waves.

LOW NEWTON-BY-THE-SEA

At Low Newton-by-the-Sea there is a splendid pub, The Ship Inn, right on the seafront. They serve tea, coffee, meals or, of course, beer.

The path now continues north-eastwards across grassland to Newton Point. It passes the lighthouse to the delightful Football Hole, a craggy inlet preceding the headland of Snook Point and wide sweep of Beadnell Bay. Everything that I said about Embleton Bay applies to Beadnell Bay. Once again we can stride forth on the luxurious bed of firm sand close to the water's edge. At Long Nanny the stride is temporarily interrupted for it is necessary to come inland to cross Brunton Burn by the footbridge.

BEADNELL

Once over it, the stroll is resumed all the way to the

Above: The wide sweep of Beadnell Bay at dusk. Below: The lime kilns and Beadnell Harbour.

twin towers which overlook Beadnell Harbour. They are in fact lime kilns.

Beadnell village lies nearly a mile distant, slightly inland. There is ample accommodation here, although there is an even wider choice at Seahouses, three miles (8km) distant.

Beadnell's harbour was built by Thomas Wood in 1797 to aid the local fishing industry and for the export of coal, salt and lime. A year later he agreed to let Richard Pringle build a kiln on his land to produce lime for use by local farmers as a fertilizer and also for export. Pringle paid Wood ninepence for every load exported and sixpence for those sold locally. New kilns were added as the operation grew. Production ceased in 1841.

ROUTE FILE

Distance	19 miles (30 km)
Time	10 hours
Terrain	Paths across pastures and cereal fields, country lanes; coastal walking across sands and fields
Accommodation	Inn & B&Bs at Craster and Beadnell; Campsites at Beadnell
Shops	P. O. at Boulmer; shops at Craster and Beadnell

13

AND SO TO LINDISFARNE

Beadnell to Holy Island

From Beadnell the route explores yet more of Northumberland's fine coastline. The fishing port of Seahouses is passed before continuing along wide, sandy beaches to Bamburgh, where the magnificent and imposing castle towers on great cliffs above the dunes and shoreline.

Across the expansive sands and mudflats of Budle Bay the abundance of bird life is there for all to see. Holy Island lies just across the water but we will have to be patient for there is no safe way along the seashore to

Beal; we have to make a short inland detour to Belford, probably a good overnight stop unless you are lucky with the tides.

Belford to Beal Sands is an easy route on rural footpaths and quiet roads. It is a preliminary to that final march across the causeway to Holy Island and as such is quick and uncomplicated. Once across the causeway you can bask in triumph for you have completed a coast-to-coast-to-coast. Now it is just a couple of miles to the picturesque village and the magic of Lindisfarne.

Bamburgh Castle from the north.

BEADNELL TO HOLY ISLAND
The Main Route

BEADNELL
The coastline north of Beadnell is laid deep with beds of limestone, coal and whin sill, inlaid with fascinating rock pools. At high tide it is prudent to regain the coastal road near the golf course in order to cross the outlet of a stream, unnamed on maps.

SEAHOUSES
The coast is regained by tracing the southern banks of the quarry pond. Otherwise circumvent the quarry pond by the Snook, skirting the golf course to reach the harbour at Seahouses.

The resort has been highly commercialized – fish and chip shops, arcades and gift shops parade themselves in the streets – it's all rather like a mini Blackpool. Trawlers congregate in the harbour – this corner of the village still exudes the aura of a working fishing port. Those interested in exploring the coast in greater detail might be interested in catching a boat from here to the Farne Islands, a sanctuary for bird life and seals.

Below: The harbour at Seahouses. Opposite: Bamburgh village and the castle.

Beyond Seahouses our route continues on the clifftops parallel to the coast road. After descending to the beach beyond St Aidan's Dunes it passes close to the dark slabs of Monk House Rocks and Greenhill Rocks. Out to sea the austere cliffs of Farne Island are plainly visible. The crags of Islestone, encountered beyond the coastguard lookout, are the roost for cormorants and shag.

BAMBURGH CASTLE
We first saw Bamburgh Castle across the waters from Seahouses. When we see it at close quarters towering above the sand dunes, its sheer size is suddenly appreciated. The impressive red sandstone fortress was built in the eleventh century on tall whin sill cliffs on the site of an earlier castle that belonged to the kings of Bernicia. At that time it would have been even closer to the sea – the sand dunes have formed since.

The castle was, for a short time, in the hands of the Scots but from 1157 onwards they were successfully resisted. During the Wars of the Roses Henry IV declared it his royal capital. Various additions have been made down the centuries making the castle a mish-mash of styles. After falling into disrepair, it was restored in Victorian times by the First Lord Armstrong.

BAMBURGH VILLAGE
The village of Bamburgh, set back from the castle and huddled round a triangular green, is well worth seeing. You probably deserve a cup of tea at one of its cafés – go on, treat yourself!

Our next stop is Belford. Although it is possible to cut a corner across inland footpaths, by far the best approach is via the northern headlands. After passing to the left of the castle and bowling green our route continues via Harkness rocks and the lighthouse to Budle Point at the head of

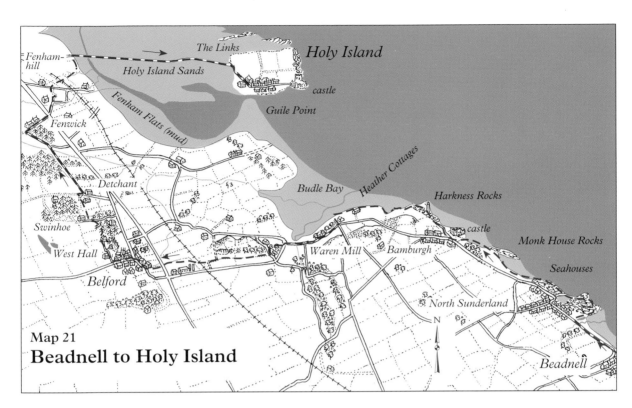

Map 21
Beadnell to Holy Island

The Laidley Worm

There's a strange tale of sorcery told in a ballad by Duncan Frazier, a thirteenth-century mountain bard of the Cheviot. It concerned a good princess by the name of Margaret, who lived a solitary life at Bamburgh Castle. Her father and brother were overseas and her mother had died. One day she received a message to say that her father was returning with a new bride and Margaret with the help of the locals and her servants prepared a grand feast of welcome.

Duly the king and his new queen arrived. The queen was beautiful but, unbeknown to the king, had been bewitched as a child. She took a dislike to the popular Princess Margaret and cast a spell on her, turning her into a Laidley Worm which was some sort of fire breathing dragon. The beast crawled away to a large cave in the Spindleston Heughs which lie to the west of Bamburgh Castle and south of Budle Bay. The king was mystified as to the disappearance of his daughter but did not suspect any foul play on his new bride's part.

Legend has it that not a blade of grass or corn would grow, so venomous was the worm's mouth. The locals were terrorized into supplying the milk of seven cows and pouring it into a stone trough at the mouth of the cave.

Word of the queen's witchcraft reached the princess's brother, who immediately set sail for England for his revenge. On reaching the Northumbrian coast he encountered a great storm lashed up by the tail of the worm's great tail. He jumped ship at Budle Bay but was greeted by the enormous monster whose fiery breath created a great sandstorm amidst the dunes. In fear the brave prince drew his sword but he heard these words:

Oh quit thy sword and bend thy bow,
And give me kisses three
For though I am a poisonous worm,
No hurt I'll do to thee.

The prince reluctantly obeyed in the traditional manner of noble princes and the spell was broken. The prince and princess confronted the queen who begged forgiveness. None was forthcoming and she was turned into a venomous toad, who fled to the basements of the castle. Some say she occasionally emerges to this day to terrorize unsuspecting tourists.

Striding along

Budle Bay. Although the golden sands of this expansive inlet look inviting do not try to make it across to Ross Links. The narrow channel of Budle Water has highly dangerous currents and lives have been lost here!

Our path continues westwards past an old concrete pier, now crumbling with the forces of the North Sea elements. It then passes in front of the weather-beaten Heather Cottages. Although it may seem strange now, for there are very few clues, this was once the site of the Borough of Warrenmouth. Founded in 1247 by Henry III as a port, it was intended to be a rival to Newcastle.

nds at Budle Bay north of Bamburgh. Do not be tempted to cross the bay for the dangerous tides and quicksands have claimed many lives over the years.

Three hundred years later the site was desolate; the project a failure.

WAREN MILL

Beyond Heather Cottages is Kiln Point (GR 153354 and not named on 1:50000 maps). Here we see the Lindisfarne Nature Reserve information sign, illustrating some of the many species of birds nesting on the mudflats. It would be unpleasant continuing much further – real welly-wallowing stuff. It is best to go southwards on the enclosed track to the road at Budle. From

the road it is still possible to peep through the hedges to see the birds. It is followed past Waren Mill to a signposted footpath at GR 145343. This follows the edge of a meadow skirting some woodland and meets a lane south of Chesterhill.

A left turn along the lane brings you to the start of a signposted footpath that heads eastwards across fields to Belford. The path closely follows the stone wall to the left of large fields, which may be planted with cereals. To the right the land rises to form squat grassy hills marked on the Pathfinder Map as Long Hills. At

Belford village centre dominated by the Blue Bell Hotel.

the time of writing no stile was provided to scale the stone wall at the end of the second field but the local authorities tell me that it will have provided one by the time we go to press.

Beyond the wall the field boundaries to the right are traced close to a large quarry to reach an enclosed lane. The lane is followed to its first bend (GR 127338). The path continues eastwards to cross a disused railway siding and onwards to cross the main Kings Cross to Edinburgh line – take extreme care. A stile and warning notice on the British Rail side mark the spot though I believe this crossing is due to be improved soon. From the railway, the path traverses fields past a grain factory to reach the next transport hazard – the A1.

BELFORD

A signposted footpath across the road points the way across more fields to Belford, passing between a golf course and a driving range to reach the outskirts of the village.

Belford was once split into two by the busy A1 but has now gained much from the new by-pass. The village centre is dominated by the church and large ivy-clad Blue Bell Inn. Unless you are lucky with the Lindisfarne tides the chances are you will be looking for accommodation. Belford offers the most with a couple of inns B&Bs and a campsite, though you can get

nearer with B&Bs at Detchant and Fenhamhill.

It's a pleasant place and maybe the last day should be a short one anyway; you do need a good deal of time to explore Holy Island fully.

ONWARDS – BACK TO THE COAST

If you did stop at Belford this will be a short final section. You will follow in the footsteps of the pilgrims across the sands to Lindisfarne Castle on Holy Island.

We *are* inland though, and we have got to make it back to the coast in time to catch the tides. I had originally hoped to make a quick return to the coast on access footpaths to Fenham Flats but found that the walking on those areas was sticky and unpleasant. Also Black Low (a coastal stream) is impassable except via the footpath inland.

From the village square by the Blue Bell Inn follow the road to Wooler. Turn right along the lane which heads north-westwards, circumventing West Hall Farm and continuing to Craggyhall. Beyond here follow a track north-westwards beneath some crags then through some delightful mixed woodlands. On reaching a wide lane turn left – this now heads to the road east of Swinhoe Farm.

DETCHANT

Take the road westwards towards Swinhoe to GR 086352 where we transfer to a public bridleway. It begins as a track which terminates at the edge of a field. A path continues vaguely, following the fence to the right, and curving north-eastwards to a gate at the top of the field. Turn right here and follow a path which soon becomes a prominent track across fields northwards to the hamlet of Detchant.

Although you will notice footpaths through the forests to the Kyloe Hills it is now better to use the quiet country lanes across the farming plains to their east. Initially the forest paths and tracks are good but to the north of Sheilow Wood they are overgrown and unpleasant to walk on. The lane is quicker and the urge will be to press on to catch that tide.

FENWICK

The lane to be used meets the busy A1 by Fenwick village. Take care with the crossing as the cars really speed hereabouts. Our route continues on the opposite side of the road on pleasant lanes, passing Fenwick Granary. Just beyond, after a twiddle in the lane, a hedge-lined track climbs to a country lane on Fenhamhill.

Turn right along the lane. After a short distance a footpath, signposted 'Goswick', is followed NNE across fields, crossing the Kings Cross to Edinburgh railway once more (take extreme care). It continues across more fields close to the shoreline on Beal Sands.

HOLY ISLAND

A stile over the fence is followed by a left turn along the coastal flats to the causeway across to Holy Island. Large concrete cubes, used to inhibit the tide, line the route.

There will be a tide timetable on a notice board at the start of the causeway. Check it with yours before preceding – just to be sure. It is a mile (1.5km) to the first dry land at The Snook and three miles (5km) to the village. The flat tarmac allows fast progress and within the hour it should all be over. Wainwright gave you a coast-to-coast; Gillham has given you a coast-to-coast-to-coast. I suppose if you do the mile to the other side of the island you would bag another coast.

Whatever you do, do not try to go straight back on the same tide. Even if you make it you will have missed the whole essence of Holy Island. When the day

Above: The little track between Fenwick Granary and Fenhamhill on the approach to the coast at Beal Sands. Below: Looking across Holy Island Sands with the Pilgrims Way marked by tall posts. You would need your wellies for this. A less sticky recommended route follows the modern causeway across the channel.

The Early Christians

Holy Island's history is inextricably linked with Christianity, a Christianity which owes much to one of its early Celtic followers, King Oswald.

After his victory at the Battle of Heavenfield (*see* Chapter 9) Oswald was proclaimed King of Northumberland and decided to spread the Word across his Kingdom. He asked the Irish monks based at St. Colomba's Iona for a teacher and Brother Gorman was sent. Unfortunately Brother Gorman was unsuccessful and, in AD635, he was replaced by Aiden.

Aiden decided to settle in Lindisfarne, as it reminded him of Iona and was also close to the Royal castle at Bamburgh. He travelled thousands of miles converting the pagans: in fact, he worked wonders and became the first of sixteen Bishops of Lindisfarne.

It is said that when he died in AD 651, a shower of stars fell from the sky. These were seen by a lowly shepherd boy from the Lammermuir Hills who asked his priest what this all meant. The priest replied that this was mourning the passing of St Aidan.

The shepherd's name was Cuthbert. He was inspired that year to join the monks at Melrose and served under Eata, one of the twelve English disciples of Aidan.

Cuthbert travelled with Eata to Lindisfarne and became Prior of Lindisfarne. In 676 he retreated to prayer and contemplation on the nearby Farne Island where he eked out a spartan existence.

On the request of King Ecfrith in 685 he returned as Bishop of Lindisfarne but within two years he was back on the Farne Island where, in 687, he died. His body was laid to rest near the altar at Lindisfarne.

In 793 the Danes ransacked the island, burning the abbey, killing many monks and looting the treasures. The abbey was rebuilt early in the next century but in 875 the monks decided to leave for Durham. They did so with many treasures including St. Cuthbert's body, the head of St Oswald, the bones of St Aidan and the Lindisfarne Gospels.

Lindisfarne meanwhile lay waste for two centuries. The monastery crumbled into ruins. After the Norman Conquest the monks fled from Durham to the island, bringing with them the shrine of St Cuthbert. After a brief period they returned to Durham. Unfortunately, it cannot be said that St Cuthbert's body has since lain in peace. The shrine was destroyed during the reformation and, although he was reburied in the same spot, his body has been exhumed in both the twelfth and nineteenth centuries by curious historians.

The Lindisfarne Gospels were written 'for God and St. Cuthbert' between 698 and 721 and contain four Gospels beautifully scripted and ornately decorated in Celtic style. They are now preserved in the British Museum.

In 1082 the priory was built. It was destroyed during the Reformation. Many of its masonry was used to build the sixteenth century castle. This was restored as a private residence in the nineteenth century by Sir Edward Lutyens and has entertained many visitors including Royalty. In 1944 it was given to the National Trust.

The statue of St Aidan, Holy Island

The sunrise behind Lindisfarne Castle, Holy Island.

trippers have left this is a wonderfully tranquil isle. Go and explore the coast, the priory, the castle; watch the sun go down behind the mainland and have a drink at one of the friendly inns or a celebration meal (you deserve it).

POSSIBLE ALTERNATIVES

The forest tracks to the Kyloe Hills by way of Swinhoe Lake and Shepherdskirk Hill would be a possible alternative to the road section from Detchant to Fenwick. Although not a right of way, there seems little resistance at present. You would have to retrace steps to Bogle House for an exit opposite Fenwick Wood.

Do *not* try sticking to the coastline beyond Budle Bay, north of Bamburgh. Deep muds and uncrossable rivers will transform your walk into a nightmare.

ROUTE FILE

Distance	22 miles (34km)
Time	10 hours*
Terrain	Varied. Coastal paths on sand , dunes & mud flats; paths across pastures and cereal fields; country lanes
Accommodation	Hotels,inns, B&Bs and campsites at Seahouses, Bamburgh, Belford and Holy Island; B&B at Detchant Farm (3 miles north of Belford), Fenwick Granary, Inn at Beal (1 mile off route from the causeway). Off-route campsite at Haggerston (3 miles north of the causeway).
Shops	Beadnell, Seahouses, Bamburgh, Belford and Holy Island

* Does not allow for the tide which will almost certainly divide this chapter into two stages. Do not take risks!

The ruins of Lindisfarne Priory.
Below: Lindisfarne Castle.

THE CHEVIOT LOOP

An Alternative High-Level Route from The Simonside Ridge to Belford

I have devised the Cheviot Loop for the fellwalkers who prefer to stick to high ground. They will substitute the Cheviots for the main Simonside Ridge, the castles of Alnwick and Bamburgh and most of the wonderful Northumbrian Heritage Coast. It is quite a sacrifice but not without its rewards.

Once out of Harwood Forest, where it departs from the main route, the Loop traverses the heather and bracken expanses of Boddle Moss on the Simonside Hills.

Descending to Hepple it samples delightful Coquetdale on farm tracks and footpaths. It visits the ancient Lady's Well and the historical villages of Holystone and Harbottle on the way to Alwinton beneath the Cheviot ridge.

The next stage uses an old drovers' road, Clennell Street, to climb to the ridge at Windy Gyle. Here you can look over a mosaic of spurs and knolls to the plains of the Scottish Borders.

The climb to the Cheviot is over heather and peat, degenerating to just peat on the summit; concrete flags now aid walkers in their efforts to stay above ground!

Dropping off the Cheviots at Cold Law, the Loop descends via the pretty Harthope Valley to Wooler. We now strike for the coast, straddling Weetwood Moor before meeting the main route near Belford.

The view eastwards from the summit of Cold Law with the heather moors rising to the Cheviot.

SECTION 1
The Harwood Forest to Alwinton

The initial section of the Cheviot route will take the word 'loop' a little too literally for some walkers. It makes a wide detour in order to take in a little of the magic of Simonside. More importantly it avoids a busy road section down the Grasslees Valley. Here you are likely to be greeted by a convoy of army trucks from the Otterburn ranges.

FALLOWLEES
From the crossroads of forestry tracks at GR 016946 in the Harwood Forest, continue straight on, following the bridleway signs to the T-junction by Chartners. From here the route climbs on another flinted track to a another T-junction near the top of the hill. Go straight on. Spruce is replaced by the more pleasing and less uniform pine. Soon the last of the conifers is left behind, and the route reaches the open fellsides of Boddle Moss. It's good to be in the light once more.

BODDLE MOSS AND WHITFIELD HILL
In views to the north, crags on Tosson Hill, the loftiest Simonside peak, crown sprawling flanks of heather,

which decline to Coquetdale's green pastures and chequered woodlands. The river valley snakes through rolling countryside before mingling with the high Cheviots. Their pale, grassy flanks seem to act as a barometer; if it's fine their sunny sides will be inviting us to hasten; if not they will reflect the blackness of the skies and warn us that it might be an idea to go to Rothbury and the coast.

The track now straddles the heathery ridge to the east of Whitfield Hill and past a shooters' hut. It is a pleasant track, although when I was last here the bulldozers were trying to scour it harder into the hillside for the 'glorious twelfth'. Views to the left towards Sandy Crags are enhanced by a wonderful tapestry. Heather, bracken, sandstone and rowan all complement each other in an ever-changing but subtle kaleidoscope. Weavers and designers of fine tweed could well benefit from this experience of nature.

HEPPLE
The track veers northwards and enters enclosed farmland to the left of a pine copse. Beyond the trees it turns half right across a field, briefly becoming less distinct. It passes in front of the large mansion of Hepple Whitfield. After briefly following its drive, a footpath signpost diverts us to the right (NE) through woodland

Tosson Hill, highest peak of the Simonside ridge, seen here from Boddle Moss at the north-western edge of the Harwood Forest.

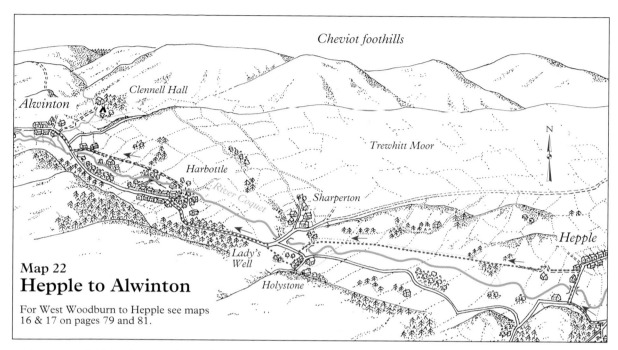

Cheviot foothills

Clennell Hall

Alwinton

N

Trewhitt Moor

Harbottle

River Coquet

Sharperton

Hepple

Map 22
Hepple to Alwinton

Lady's
Well

Holystone

For West Woodburn to Hepple see maps
16 & 17 on pages 79 and 81.

and across a field to the next farm. A track to the left behind the farmhouse continues to a minor road.

Turn left along the road to meet the B road then right to cross the bridge over the Coquet. A short way beyond, and just short of Hepple's village centre, a met-alled track, signposted 'Border County Ride', is fol-lowed eastwards to West Hepple Hall. Once past the farm, the tarmac ceases and is replaced by a pleasant and well-way-marked farm track running NNW parallel to the River Coquet. You are looking down the length of the valley now, with the afforested foothills of the Otterburn hills on one side and rolling pastureland on the other. The high Cheviot ridge runs the length of the northern skyline.

HOLYSTONE

At GR 958032 cross the wooden footbridge over the Coquet. A path from the other side leads to the road just north of Holystone, where the excellent Salmon Inn offers refreshments and meals.

It is quicker here to follow the quiet lanes to Harbottle but many may wish to visit Lady's Well on a slight detour from the village centre. The path from the well heads northwards across fields and back to the road at Wood Hall. (NB The bridleway shown from the bridge at Sharperton, GR 954038, to Peels Farm is

impassable. It is blocked by a fence at the start and the wide and deep river crossing which has no bridge, would be extremely dangerous.)

HARBOTTLE

Harbottle has two castles. The old and more historically

Holystone

Holystone was founded in the twelfth century and grew up around the priory of Augustinian nuns that survived until the sixteenth century. The only reminder of the priory is the tiny church of St Mary and much of this was renovated in the nineteenth century.

The village is probably best known for Lady's Well, a rectangular pool enshrouded by trees and fed by crystal-clear spring water. It has a stone cross mounted in the middle and a statue of St Paulinus at its side. St Paulinus is said to have baptized over 3,000 Northumbrians during Easter AD627. Lady's Well is now owned by the National Trust.

Holystone is on an old Roman road which straddled the moorland wilderness to the west and served the forts at Chew Green and High Rochester. The legions may well have used the old well.

On the track between Harbottle and Alwinton with the Simonside Hills on the horizon.
Below: On Clennell Street descending the slopes of Yarnspath Law towards Usway Burn.

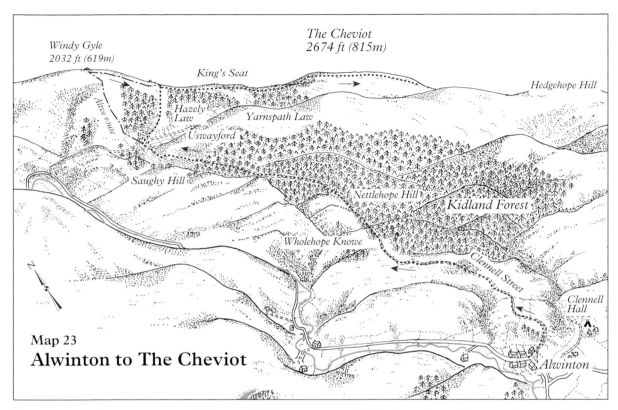

Map 23
Alwinton to The Cheviot

important one is now a ruin and lies perched on a grassy mound to the north of the main road. It was built in 1160 for Henry II and the Bishop of Durham. The grandmother of James I of England was born here in 1515. The second castle, which is still intact, was built in the nineteenth century for use as a shooting lodge using stones from the original fortress. It lies to the east of the village close to the River Coquet and is now a private house and craft centre.

Having spent two miles (3km) on tarmac it is pleasant to get off the road again. At Harbottle's eastern end follow the lane towards the modern castle then turn left to cross the Coquet by way of a footbridge next to a ford – the footbridge is hidden at first, don't panic! A track now climbs parallel to the river and past a cottage onto high pastures. There are good views down the valley and across to the heather hills of Harbottle. A study of the contours on the map tells us that these are special hills but the army got here first and they are largely out of bounds.

Beyond Park House Farm the track is metalled but is delightfully lined with many species of wild flower – a

colourful sight in spring and summer. It descends to the road, passing some large lime kilns and the church at Low Alwinton.

ALWINTON
Alwinton proper is a short distance along the road. The peaceful village lies on a wide plain close to the confluence of the rivers Coquet and Alwin and is sheltered by hills on all four sides. There's a campsite at Clennell Hall and a chance for more refreshment at the Rose and Thistle. Being a border inn, the rose signifies the rose of England and the thistle is that of Scotland.

SECTION 2
Alwinton to Wooler

ALWINTON AND CLENNELL STREET
Clennell Street will now be our route to the hills. The old drove road begins from the green at GR 923063 and climbs onto the grassy hillsides overlooking the valley of the River Alwin. After passing the farm of

Clennell Street

Although it is a known medieval drove road, Clennell Street's origins are believed to be much older – it was possibly a prehistoric trade route and would almost certainly have been used by the Romans.

Straddling the Cheviot ridge at Windy Gyle, it linked the villages of Alwinton and Cocklawfoot, although taking its name form the once flourishing village of Clennell.

Herds of sheep and cattle would be driven along the road from Scotland southward to Morpeth, Newcastle and maybe the markets of Yorkshire: herds of up to a 1000 sheep and 200 cattle were not unusual..

During the turbulent centuries of warfare between England and Scotland the route was used by the murderous Border Reivers, who would plunder cattle from the fearful rural population. Later it is said that Clennell Street became a devious route for whisky smugglers sneaking into England the back way. Like most drovers' roads Clennell Street was overtaken by the passage of time – traffic was diverted onto the railway and the turnpike road.

Clennellstreet (the Northumbrians have a habit of joining words together), the road climbs towards the dense plantations of the Kidland Forest and enters them on Wholehope Hill. The darkness is short lived, however, and we emerge on Saughy Hill with new views across wild, reedy moors to the Cheviot ridge.

On Nettlehope Hill there is a fork in the tracks. We take the one to the left, which re-enters the spruce-woods and turns north-westwards (the one to the right goes to the B&B at Uswayford Farm, pronounced oosy-ford). Once again the street escapes from the clutches of the Forestry Commission and descends into the valley of Usway Burn. Windy Gyle can clearly be seen on the skyline.

USWAY BURN

A footbridge conveys the route across the burn and we climb northwards to a stile in a fence. Don't be enticed onto a path on the northern banks of the stream - it is rougher and certainly no short cut.

Beyond the stile, our path climbs westwards to meet the track between Middle Hill and Hazely Law. Turn right along it and, unless you want B&B at Uswayford Farm (GR 886145), continue northwards close to the eastern boundaries of the Hepden Burn spruce woods.

NB For those wanting a direct route NW to Windy Gyle, the bridleway shown on the map is not signposted or well-used. There are also confusing military signs. It *is* usable though. Cross Hepden Burn on a grassy track signposted to Trows then turn right on a slightly less prominent grassy rake to reach a flinted track. Go straight across on rough pastures following the southern edge of the conifer plantation. The route does not enter them (as it does on the map) but continues on the western perimeter for a couple of hundred yards then climbs north-westwards across rough moorland skirting the south-western edge of Little Ward Law. It follows a stream for a while then, at GR861148, it crosses the stream and climbs to a gate on the ridge to the west of Windy Gyle's summit.

Opposite: Russells Cairn on the summit at Windy Gyle. Below: Usway Burn

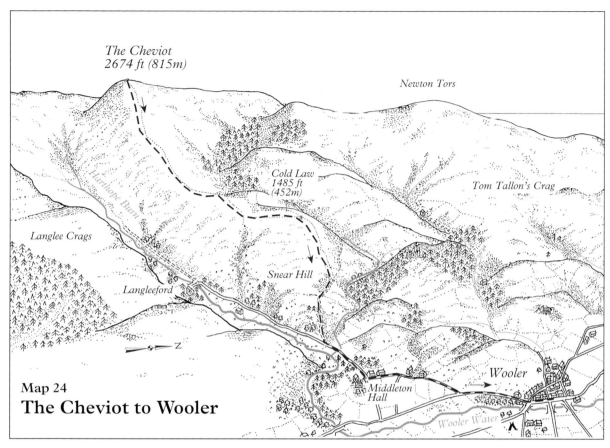

Map 24
The Cheviot to Wooler

THE CHEVIOT RIDGE

The bridleway used by the more direct route climbs to the northern summit of Hazley Law then attains the ridge at GR 872161 between Windy Gyle and Kings Seat. Hardy souls may want to make a detour to the former, both for the views and to see Russell's Cairn. The cairn is said to commemorate Lord Francis Russell, who was killed here in 1585. Many historians argue that it is a Bronze Age burial mound.

The summit is a superb place to be on a clear day. It has good views in all directions – the Cheviot looms large beyond the heathland of Kings Seat and Cairn Hill and the deep nick of Rowhope Burn plots a meandering course through velvet-draped grassy knolls.

A short distance east on the descent from Windy Gyle is another cairn, said by some to be the true Russell's Cairn.

CAIRN HILL

The path continues along the route of the Pennine Way over rough, heather-clad peatlands to Kings Seat. Here the long, arduous ascent to Cairn Hill begins. The ground can be horribly boggy after periods of rain but the going is made easier by the gradual addition of board walks. To many, including myself, these are alien to wilderness country, but, at this stage in the proceedings, few travellers will be grumbling.

At a fence corner (GR 897194), two Pennine Way alternative routes divert. The one to the north heads towards Kirk Yetholm via Auchope Cairn and the Schil, whilst the one to the east, which we should follow, heads for The Cheviot.

THE CHEVIOT

The very worst of the treacherous path has been paved and thus the sting has been taken out of this Cheviot's tail. The summit's trig point lies in the midst of the porridge. Since the first construction in the last century, two trig points have been lost in the peat. The present one has been supported by an 11ft (3.3m) pile and now it's the hill that is sinking (erosion of the peat surface). The Cheviot affords good views of the Northumberland coastline and distant 'Border' hills but the expansiveness of the massif restricts more intimate views of the valley complexes.

From the summit the path continues ('paved' for a short distance at the time of writing) across horrible peat mires. Things improve on descending towards Scald Hill. The views of the Harthope Valley are

probably the finest views since leaving the Lake District. Hedgehope Hill's well-rounded profile reminds me of a Christmas pudding, the outlines of its summit peat hags resembling the dripping sauce. The path is still marshy in places but nothing to dampen the spirits. For a short distance there are firm grassy slopes. The wide expanses of chequered pasture and little hills of coastal Northumbria lead the eye to the faint blue

Dining out on the eastern slopes of The Cheviot with Hedgehope Law in the mid-distance and the coastal plains fading to the distant coast.

stretch of the North Sea and we feel our mission is almost accomplished. Descending from this lofty perch with the world beneath one's feet is the nearest thing to flying when carrying a thirty-pound rucksack.

After briefly climbing to the grassy summit of Scald Hill the route follows the ridge towards Broadhope Hill. The Valley of Lambden Burn opens up to the left, with the lonely Goldscleugh farm lying sandwiched between patches of spruce woods and the crowding flanks of the Cheviot.

COLD LAW

Ignore the east-west footpath which straddles the heather-clad ridge by a gate in the fence at GR 935230 but continue to the fence corner south of Broadhope Hill's summit. Turn right and follow the ridge here to

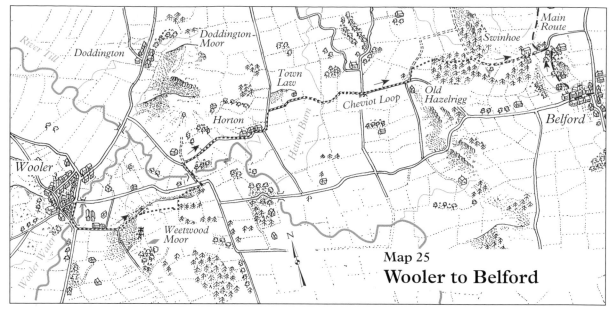

Map 25
Wooler to Belford

Cold Law, where a short detour southward leads to the trig point and stone shelter on the true top. This is an excellent viewpoint. On the far side of the Harthope Valley the rock-fringed ridge swells to shapely Hedgehope Hill and still further to the big Cheviot. Looking northward across towards Yeavering Bell reveals a more barren landscape of windswept, grassy moorland. Some day I will come back to see what Tom Tallon's Crag looks like.

WOOLER

From Cold Law continue by the ridge fence and past a couple of crags to meet the track from Broadstruther. This now descends Snear Hill on a spur dividing the Harthope Valley and the ravine of Carey Burn. From here country lanes lead past Earle into Wooler. This lively market town is tightly tucked between hills on the southern edge of the flat plains of the Rivers Glen and Till.

SECTION 3
Wooler to Belford (Swinhoe)

WEETWOOD MOOR
It's time to head for the coast. Our route takes us across the busy A697 road to the east of the village and

continues on Brewery Lane, so called because the St Magnus Brewery was once sited here. Hops still grow in the hedge near the farm.

The lane climbs onto Weetwood Moor and is left at a sharp bend. A track enclosed by thickets now continues uphill. About hundred yards (70m) beyond a gate the track is left for a grooved path, way-marked by an arrow. It rakes to the right onto the moorland plateau with fine views back to the Cheviots and north-wards to Doddington Law.

The path is clear until criss-crossed by a few other routes. Go left at the first crossroads (you will notice a marker post on the unwanted track that continues straight on). Twenty yards further is another five-way junction. It's slightly right of straight on this time on an ENE route over bracken and heather.

Beyond a gate we enter pastureland with a pine forest directly ahead. Turn left beyond a gate by the western end of this plantation and follow the fence downhill to a small gate in a grassy hollow. The hollow declines to sheltered fields beneath the northern slopes of the moor. A narrow path now leads to the right and threads between gorse bushes to a roadside five-bar gate close to the bridge over the River Till.

HORTON AND HAZELRIGG
Turn left along the road for a few yards then cross the

fine stone bridge. The lane twists beneath the flanks of Doddington Law and is followed past the adjoining farming hamlets of West and East Horton.

To the north at GR 029313 a metalled farm lane to the right is taken. It climbs the pastured slopes of Town Law, capped with a few pines. After a mile, the road degenerates into a stony track and descends to cross Hetton Burn. It then rakes to the left to climb out to a country lane opposite the old schoolhouse at Hazelrigg (GR 049328). Go straight on to the 108m spot height past the T-junction near Old Hazelrigg

Above: On Weetwood Moor, looking back to Wooler and the Cheviots. Below left: Weetwood Bridge.

farm before turning left on a farm track signposted to 'Swinhoe and Holburn'. This climbs past an old quarry shortly before being abandoned at a gate to the right at the top of the 'hill'.

The path follows the edge of a field. Beyond the first five-bar gate a right turn is made towards the forest, which is entered via a ladder stile or the adjacent gate.

The devious path through this forest is way-marked by yellow arrows. The route is not exactly the same as that of the map and you will have to keep your eyes open. It follows a series of rides and narrow paths through the trees. Generally the direction is north-east-wards veering eastwards in the middle stages. Keep to the path for these are privately owned forests. Close to the exit from the plantation the substantial ruins of a kiln are passed.

SWINHOE

On leaving the forest, take the track 'to Swinhoe' which runs straight as a die past the strangely named Old Dickwalls Farm. Beyond Swinhoe turn left on the path described in the main route (*see* Chapter 13).

ROUTE FILE

Distance	
Elsdon to Holy Island	56 miles (91 kms)
Time	30 hours (3/4 days)
Terrain	A mixture of forest and riverside paths in early stages then a climb on good tracks to the Cheviot ridge. The marshy ridge is gradually being made easier by the addition of stone slabs
Accommodation	Inn and B&Bs at Holystone, Harbottle and Alwinton. Campsites at Alwinton and Belford. See Chapter 13 for accommodation beyond Belford
Shops	Belford and Holy Island

NICOLA'S DIARY

Our First Lakeland to Lindisfarne Crossing

by Nicola Gillham

When you marry a man who writes walking books for a living it helps if you enjoy walking. I do, but I had never done a long distance walk.

John's first suggestion was that we should backpack – take a tent and camp along the way, if possible on the tops. I said no but, after much discussion, I agreed to a long distance walk. We would stop at B&Bs each night and limit the daily travel to a reasonable (for me) number of miles.

I sent for all the accommodation brochures from the tourist offices along the way. John then planned the route with stopping places. All the B&B s were booked, deposits paid and there was no turning back.

Friday 7th May 1993
We left home at lunchtime after a hectic morning at work and arrived at Ravenglass at 8.00 on a beautiful Spring evening. Being slightly superstitious I was a bit worried about a big cloud that covered the sun just as we stepped off the train.

Rosegarth Guest House turns out to be surprisingly nice. Our room overlooks the sea and is very pretty.

Saturday 8th May
I woke up early with anticipation but my spirits sank when I saw the clouds outside. Breakfast is superb though – with fresh fruit salad served with the muesli followed by bacon, eggs and all the trimmings. We left Rosegarth with the sun shining. We are raring to go but first the obligatory photograph. I cannot dip my feet in the sea – the tide's out!

The walk starts along the beach. We've been here before so there is no need for route-finding. Not that I do anyway. I arrange appropriate food and accommodation and carry as little as possible. Soon we were

walking through lovely woods and hedgerows with bluebells, primroses and lots of rhododendrons. Muncaster Fell gave us our first glimpse of the big mountains and it was easy walking down to Eskdale, which had toilets and a shop selling almost everything, including ice cream.

The bit out of Eskdale is quite steep but John said we could have lunch on top (he knows how to bribe me). We met some people halfway up who asked for directions. John put them right and they turned round and walked back the way they had come. It's amazing the number of people we see with no map and no idea of their whereabouts.

We arrived at the ridge and had lunch overlooking Nether Wasdale. It is all flat or downhill after this final rise. The rest of the walk is lovely along the top of the screes and down into Wasdale Head. It was cloudy by this time, but the views down to the lake and Wasdale Head were superb.

We arrived at the pub at 4.30 – plenty of time for a refreshing lager before finding our B&B for the night. It was easy to find, just round the corner from the pub – how convenient. Inside it looked a bit spartan and even I could have made a better job of the wall papering though I won't tell John that. The beef stew and dumplings was just what the doctor ordered after a day's walking.

Amazingly we both felt the need for an after-dinner stroll and we walked down the valley on the route we would take the following day.

Sunday 9th May
Another beautiful day, though rather windy. Actually there was one cloud in the sky and of course the cloud was where we were going. It was a long, hard pull up to

Sty Head Pass into the wind but the scenery got better and better. So far there were no aches and pains from the journey. John hadn't told me it was uphill again after Sprinkling Tarn but it didn't matter as my legs were working well. I think I've found another of my favourite places.

Our journey continued eventually down to the Old Dungeon Gill via the pony track at Rossett Gill. The question was, could we make it before closing time at 3.00. Given that incentive my legs came alive and we made it with half an hour to spare. We were lucky – some musicians were playing the Eagles songs in the beer garden and we had a relaxing half hour listening to them.

Relaxing at the Old Dungeon Ghyll Hotel, Great Langdale. Photo: Nicola Gillham

It was an awfully long way down the valley to Elterwater – nearly flat and very pleasant, but still a long way. My legs were tiring. I think the 'twice round the block' training was not quite enough.

Elterwater is a lovely little place with a nice-looking pub but, what a disappointment, the road sign said 4 miles to Ambleside, our destination. It was time for drastic action – change the socks and eat the last chocolate biscuit. I did suggest chocolate fudge cake at the gift shop in Skelwith Bridge but John said no – he was route finding at the time – not a good time to suggest anything.

I did think Loughrigg Fell was a bit much - uphill on the last part of the day. I had my trainers on for comfort but the going was still tough for my little legs. At last Ambleside and civilization but where was the Thorneyfield Guest House? Luckily for John it was easy to find and on the right side of town. Now where is the bathroom? What a calamity, no plug for the bath – I'll have to make do with a shower. My legs had stiffened up. I could only just hobble out for a bar meal but you will not catch me missing out on food.

Monday 10th May
I woke up early. It's the third day and I was told that we should have planned for an easy day because the effects of the first two will have caught up with me. John says

it's about the same length as yesterday – my heart sank, my legs felt very stiff.

The sky was overcast and it looked like rain. I began to have second thoughts about bringing the lightweight waterproof – will it *be* waterproof?

We are on the way by 9.30 having called at the chemist for pain killers and fiery jack (just in case). We soon had our waterproofs on but I enjoyed the walk over to Troutbeck. It was nice and leisurely and not difficult at all. The track up to the Garburn Pass was much steeper and I'd a feeling I had got the third-day syndrome. My right leg hurt every time I lifted my foot and we had only done 6 miles. John proposed a slight change of plan; from Kentmere we would go over the Nan Bield Pass and down to Haweswater – only one more hill instead of two.

The scenery was beautiful but I was concentrating on putting one foot in front of the other. At last we reached the pass. It's all down hill from here and the high winds that had developed would be at our backs. But we are way behind schedule; it's 4.00 and John reckoned that, at this pace, we would make Bampton Grange by 8.00. Aaagh! That meant it was a long way and I was very tired.

I changed into trainers for the walk down the side of Haweswater – 7 miles to Bampton Grange. We opted for the right-hand side – it's on the road but the Haweswater Hotel is halfway along. They had some splendid old pictures of the valley before it was flooded for the reservoir. We could have stopped here but it was £22.50 for B&B so I had chosen the Crown & Mitre at Bampton Grange at £15.00, a decision I now regretted.

The road seems to last for ever but eventually as the church clock struck 8.00 we entered Bampton Grange. Now the questions were – could I get upstairs and had they got a deep bath? The answer to both was yes.

Tuesday 11th May
John had promised an easy day today and it was; leisurely walking along country lanes and gentle paths. We had fancied a refreshing drink at one of Morland's two pubs but they were closed so we pressed on. The last couple of miles to Temple Sowerby are along the banks of the River Eden so of course I had to have a paddle – lovely!

We arrived early at Temple Sowerby and found the B&B facing the village green. Mrs Jephcott was very friendly and made us tea and biscuits when we arrived – very welcome as we'd had no lunch.

Wednesday 12th May
Breakfast was enormous. Mrs J had taken my remark of no lunch seriously and provided enough food to last us all day. I caught the sun yesterday and now have red legs and a red nose – no need to worry today, though, for it's cloudy and very windy.

Today we went up Cross Fell and down to Garrigill. It was a longer walk than yesterday, but there was the George and Dragon and sticky toffee pudding to look forward to. The Helm Wind was blowing on Cross Fell and it's two steps forward and one back. One packet of crisps between two is all we need. We said hello to some Pennine Wayers near Greg' Hut and then met them again later in the pub. I'm feeling much fitter than two days ago and the final 7 miles to Garrigill were quite easy.

The George and Dragon was locked when we arrived and we had to hammer on the door! They said they were expecting us yesterday – I don't think I got it wrong! We had a really good night in the bar, and struck up a conversation with some people doing the Pennine Way the hard way (with a tent) and also a couple doing the Alternative Pennine Way. John's *Pennine Ways* was not out then so we forgave them.

Thursday 13th May
Excellent breakfast as usual at the George & Dragon.

Today we would walk to Allendale Town, about 15 miles away. 'It should be quite easy,' says John – he said that about Ambleside to Bampton Grange. I had forebodings about today for some reason – perhaps it was the grey sky and the mist, low over the hills.

Sure enough it was soon raining and we were on compass bearings over the moor to Nenthead. We walked the country roads to Coalcleugh. It's now raining very hard. A mini bus from an outdoor centre in Allenheads stopped to offer us a lift. 'What a good idea,' I think, but John, being an experienced long distance walker, wouldn't hear of it.

We reached Allendale at about 5.00, very wet and bedraggled. The Heatherlea Hotel looked very large and imposing and we found a bus shelter to change from our boots and water proofs. It was lovely inside but Mrs Bucher says we are not expected. I could not understand; I confirmed everything in writing. Luckily there was plenty of room – in fact the place was empty and we were given the best room in the house. It was newly decorated and carpeted throughout but with nowhere to put our wet boots, waterproofs and rucksacks – even the bathroom has carpet. We slept well in a four poster bed.

Friday 14th May
We couldn't believe it when we woke up to snow, yes snow. We declined another lift and set off in pouring rain to walk the 10 miles to Hexham.

The moors were thick with snow and mist. I wondered how good John was at route finding for the tracks were non-existent under all that white stuff. The bighead ended up in exactly the right place though and we continued on lanes which were transformed into streams by the continuous rainfall and melting snow. The verges were the driest place to walk. I cannot imagine why, but both John and I were really enjoying ourselves, battling against the elements. Some of the river crossings were hmm, entertaining.

We arrived in Hexham about 3.00, very wet but pleased that we had triumphed over the elements. The Station Hotel looked just as I expected, grim and uninviting. It had been one of John's choices, of course; somehow he had imagined as an ivy-clad country town type inn. Inside was better than I had expected and at least it was warm and dry.

Saturday 15th May
Mum and Dad arrived for the weekend bringing me my

Goretex waterproof and some more clothes, This was a rest day and being driven for an evening bar meal was a luxury.

Sunday 16th May

This was our shortest day yet. Mum and Dad decided to accompany us and then get a taxi back to Hexham.

Route finding is always a bit problematical with my dad along. He works on the principle of following his nose. This is OK if you don't need anybody else to follow the route later.

We arrived at the Barrasford Arms before closing time and had a beer in the garden before waving goodbye to mum and dad.

Nicola bathing her feet in the River Eden.

Monday 17th May

We left Barrasford at 9.00 after an excellent breakfast. I'm not sure about these cooked breakfasts. I might be fitter at the end of this walk but will I also be fatter?

Today's walk is pleasant enough but hasn't got the splendour of the Lakes or Cross Fell. I don't think the day off was a good idea. I seem to have lost some of the momentum. It didn't help when it started to rain.

We arrived in Otterburn very tired and very wet. Both pairs of boots are soaking but John's are in a very poor state. The Butterchurn guest house was very welcoming and our room had a tiled en-suite bathroom – just right for drying all our wet things. Too late to book a bar meal. We ate at the palatial Otterburn Hall.

Tuesday 18th May

Today we head for Rothbury via Elsdon and the Simonside Hills. I've seen some of this area before and I'm looking forward to it. The sun came out today and we got our first view of the sea. It was quite something to think that I had nearly walked across the country.

It was a long day but really enjoyable – what a difference a bit of sun makes. The Queens Head in Rothbury was very good. We had a whole floor to ourselves, two bathrooms and a separate toilet. I think a bath rather than a shower is a definite plus point when on a long distance walk.

Wednesday 19th May

I'm writing this on Friday, it's the first time I have felt like picking up a pen. It's been a hard couple of days. Rothbury to Alnwick proved to be tiring and frustrating. The route out along the river was lovely but as soon as we hit the footpaths through the fields we hit trouble. No large-scale map and no compass (somebody lost it!) made route finding difficult. Further on the bridleway through the forest does not exist underfoot and we ended up pushing our way through spruce trees. As if this wasn't enough for one day we encountered barbed wire fences obstructing the footpath at Edlingham. John says he will have to come again to change this section.

There were some better moments at the castle and church at Edlingham. They were well worth a visit and it wasn't raining (not then anyway). A final torrential rainfall and a field full of cow pats accompanied our entry into Alnwick.

Thursday 20th May

This should have been a fairly easy day, the coast was within striking distance and there were no hills along the way. The day started well with a walk along the river opposite the castle. I'd like to come back and have a look inside when we have more time. Oh, I forgot to mention John threw his boots in the bin before we left. They were in a bit of a state but I do think he could have removed the nice, new red laces I'd bought for him before we started the walk.

The fields near the coast were a bit of a problem with long grass and oil-seed rape – not very pleasant. At last we reached the coast. There was just time to have a paddle in the sea before it started raining again. We'd planned to have kippers in Craster but when we arrived the café was closed. Beer and sandwiches in the pub had to suffice.

The walk along the coast was wonderful; Dunstanburgh Castle and long empty beaches. Approaching Beadnell I began to have doubts as to the exact whereabouts of tonight's B&B, the Shepherd's Rest. I think she said straight on past the harbour. Beadnell turned out to be a long narrow village and the B&B very elusive. We found a telephone box and rang for directions. It was at the other side of the village about a mile away – and uphill! I take full responsibility for this slight error.

We arrived eventually at 7.00 wet through, cold and hungry. I asked the lady if she could provide us with some sandwiches to save us from going out in the rain the nearest pub was a mile away. I was rather surprised when she said sorry she had no bread. Her husband was watching the football so he couldn't run us down to the village in his car. There was nothing for it but to don our waterproofs and walk back down to the village.

Friday 21st May

It seemed amusing when we were offered more toast at breakfast time. I wonder where the bread came from?

Thankfully it was not raining although very misty. It was good to be on the move. I felt as though we were getting near journey's end. I am starting to think about how we will get to Lindisfarne and how we will get home.

We ambled along the beach passing through Seahouses, a smaller version of Blackpool. It seems out of place in this lovely landscape.

We almost walked past Bamburgh Castle in the thick mist. Its imposing outlines suddenly loomed through the murk. It was lunch time so we wandered into the village and bought cakes and coffee before continuing to Budle Bay, a large inlet. We could see Lindisfarne just across the water but without a boat it would be tomorrow before we reached it.

Mud replaced sand on the coastline and we reluctantly left the coast and turned inland for Belford. I'd booked us into the Bluebell Farmhouse which was supposed to be very near to the centre of the village. After yesterdays fiasco I told John to guard the rucksacks while I explored.

The farmhouse turned out to be a modern design detached house on the outskirts of a campsite but, as promised, it was very near the centre of the village. We were made very welcome with tea and biscuits and advice on where to go for our evening bar meal.

Saturday 22nd May

We had to make an early start because of the tides: we must reach the causeway by 1.00 and it's about 9 miles. Other guests had arrived last night and they were very interested to hear about our journey so the early start got somewhat delayed. Another problem was that the planned route was possibly blocked, according to our landlady. After taking advice over the phone from our landlady's friend, we decided to walk along the road and find a better route next time.

The journey was not very pleasant but quickly forgotten as we headed for the coast and our final destination – Holy Island. The sun shone brightly for our last day and I felt on top of the world. We arrived and had a celebratory half of lager before touring the island. As the tide turned the crowds melted away and we were left to share the essence of Lindisfarne with the birds and a few locals.

Our final B&B was Rose Cottage and we were given a lovely room with windows on two sides overlooking the sea. What a romantic place to end our walk.

To celebrate we booked a table in a local restaurant, North View Lodge. The meal was excellent – with wine, liqueurs etc. The proprietor, Alan Robertson, offered us a lift back across the causeway tomorrow. This means we can have a last look round in the morning without the worry of missing the bus to Newcastle.

Looking back a year later, I feel that Lakeland to Lindisfarne was a real achievement. There were times when my legs ached and I was wet through but there were also times of elation. I enjoyed the scenery, the people we met along the way and the sense of anticipation wondering what each day would bring. Lakeland to Lindisfarne will not be my last long-distance walk.

Appendix

SAFETY AND PLANNING

Although I have split the main route into thirteen sections it is not a recommended schedule for all. Experienced long-distance walkers would easily be able to cover these distances but it is best to choose the itinerary to match *your* preferred pace.

It is advisable to book accommodation well in advance. This is especially true in the summer months when the smaller establishments quickly fill up. I have not compiled an accommodation list as I did for Snowdonia to Gower or the Bowland-Dales Traverse. Experience tells me that they date too quickly. Contact the tourist information centres (*see* box) – they are always glad to help and will send an accommodation list.

When booking your accommodation it is always best to advise the landlord/landlady that you are on foot and may be late arriving; that way they should not give your room to somebody else. Nicola tells me to mention that it is good if they have a bath rather than a shower. It *is* nice to have a good soak after hard day on the fells.

TIME TO GO?

The best time to tackle Lakeland to Lindisfarne is probably in June or July. Daylight hours are at their longest and the climate is milder with a greater likelihood of some sunshine.

Many long-distance walkers like to set off in May. Spring flowers are blooming in the meadows and the contrast between the rust-red bracken and the trees' new green foliage can be striking. But frost and snow is still possible at this time; campers would have to pack their bulkiest sleeping bags and extra warm clothes. High-mountain walkers may, at this time, need their crampons and ice-axes to reach the Lakeland tops. More often than not at this time of the year, the terrain hasn't quite dried out – there may be an added squelch to your walk.

In August and September it can be wet and, although your walk is perfectly legal, your peace may be disturbed by a grouse-shooting party. In the winter months daylight hours are too limited to achieve much

distance. Unless you are an experienced winter mountain walker it is better to stick to spring and summer.

EQUIPMENT AND SAFETY

I am not going to cover this section in detail. There are some books such as Clive Tully's *Trail Walking Handbook* and Chris Townshend's *The Backpacker's Handbook*, which cover the subject far better than I could. Magazine articles and reviews in say *Trail Walker* or *Great Outdoors* are also useful.

The main Lakeland to Lindisfarne route is probably comparable in difficulty to Wainwright's Coast to Coast and certainly easier on the feet than the Pennine Way. It is still a serious expedition and should not be underestimated.

The successful long-distance walker should be reasonably fit although you do not have to be in the first flush of youth or a marathon runner. Build up your fitness gradually. Try doing long day-walks, then a lengthy weekend itinerary, complete with the gear you expect to take on the main trip. It is no use planning a schedule of fifteen miles a day on a long-distance walk if the most you have ever done before is ten; this will almost certainly lead to difficulties.

It is extremely important that all hillwalkers are fully practised in the use of map and compass. Their lives depend on it. If the mist comes down on the mountain it is essential that you know exactly where you are and the direction required to get safely off the mountain.

Make sure you take enough food and water – keep some additional emergency rations in the corner of the rucksack. The average adult male walker needs about 4,000 calories each day; far more than you would need for a day at the office. Many people eat a lot of sweet things but, although some sugar is good for fast-releasing energy, starchy foods containing complex carbohydrates are the most important. These are contained in the likes of bread and potatoes. Eat some fat too – nuts and dairy products etc.

You'll need plenty of water, especially on hot days when the body perspires a lot. It is very easy and very

PLANNING CHART

DISTANCES

stage	from start miles	km	Comments
Ravenglass	0	0	
Eskdale Green	6	9	
Nether Wasdale *	*9*	*13*	
Wasdale Head	14	22	
Old Dungeon Gill Hotel	21	34	
Elterwater	25	41	
Ambleside	28	46	
Troutbeck	32	52	
Kentmere	37	58	
Haweswater Hotel *	*45*	*70*	
Bampton Grange	48	77	
Morland	55	87	
Temple Sowerby	59	93	
Kirkland	63	100	
Garrigill	71	115	
Nenthead	74	120	
Allenheads *	*80*	*130*	*via road from Coalcleugh*
Allendale Town	84	137	
Whitley Chapel	90	147	
Hexham	94	153	
Acomb	95	156	
Chollerford	100	161	
Barrasford	102	164	
Birtley	106	171	
Wark *	*107*	*173*	
Redesmouth	109	176	
Bellingham *	*111*	*179*	
West Woodburn	114	184	
Elsdon	120	193	
Rothbury	133	214	
Edlingham	144	232	
Alnwick	151	243	
Lesbury	156	251	
Alnmouth *	*157*	*253*	
Boulmer	159	256	
Craster	162	261	
Beadnell	169	273	
Seahouses	171	276	
Bamburgh	175	283	
Waren Mill	178	287	
Belford	180	291	
Detchant	183	295	
Fenwick	187	301	
Holy Island (village)	192	310	

The Cheviot Loop

Elsdon	120	193	
Hepple	133	215	
Holystone	136	219	
Harbottle	138	222	
Alwinton	140	225	
Uswayford Farm *	*146*	*235*	
Wooler	158	255	
Main route at Swinhoe	167	269	(N of Belford)
Holy Island (village)	176	284	

NB Places marked with an asterisk are off route but may offer useful accommodation.

ORDNANCE SURVEY MAPS FOR THE ROUTES

1:50000 Landranger Series :-
Nos 89, 90, 91, 87, 80, 81 and 75
Useful Outdoor Leisure Maps (1:25000) which cover some of the route are Nos 5, 6, 7 and 31 . These would replace Landrangers 89 and 90.

TRANSPORT

Ravenglass is served by British Rail and can be reached via Barrow or Carlisle. There is a bus off Holy Island stopping at the A1 at Beal. You can get another bus to Newcastle or Berwick from here. Both are on the London Kings Cross to Edinburgh railway line. For those who want to get to the North-West, trains run from Newcastle direct to Manchester Liverpool and Carlisle.

TIDE TIMETABLES

The Holy Island crossing timetables are essential for Lakeland to Lindisfarne. They can be obtained from the Tourist Information Centre at The Shambles, Alnwick, Northumberland NE66 1TN. Tel: 01665 510665.

YOUTH HOSTELS

Nether Wasdale, Wastwater, 2 miles off route - Whin Rigg, High Close, Elterwater
Ambleside
Waterhead
Alston, 4 miles off route from Garrigill
Acomb, Nr Hexham
Bellingham, 2 miles off route at Redesmouth
Rock, inland from Craster on the Northumberland coast.
Wooler on the Cheviot Loop

TOURIST INFORMATION CENTRES
(Year-round opening)

For Ravenglass to Wasdale Head:-
Civic Centre, Lowther Street, WHITEHAVEN, Cumbria CA28 7DG. Tel: 01946 695678

For Langdale to Kentmere:-
Victoria Street, WINDERMERE, Cumbria LA23 1AD. Tel: 019662 6499

For Haweswater to Allendale Town:-
Robinson's School, PENRITH, Cumbria CA11 7PT. Tel: 01768 67466

For Dalton (north of Hexham) to Elsdon:-
The Manor Office, Hallgate, HEXHAM, Northumberland NE46 1XD. Tel: 0434 605225

For Rothbury to Craster:-
The Shambles, ALNWICK, Northumberland Tel: 01665 510665

From Beadnell to Holy Island:-
Castlegate Car Park, BERWICK-UPON-TWEED, Northumberland TD15 1JS. Tel: 01289 330733

dangerous to become seriously dehydrated. Fast flowing mountain streams usually contain good fresh water, fit for drinking. You can buy water purification tablets for extra security though they add an unpleasant taste. Also check a short way upstream for anything untoward that could pollute the water supply – like a dead sheep.

Some water you just don't need – rain. Good waterproofs are essential. Modern breathable fabrics such as those made with Goretex, Cyclone and Sympatex linings are generally regarded as the best. I do know some walkers, however, who prefer to go for the non-breathable types, which are much cheaper, lighter and more compact. Unfortunately the condensation that forms on the inside of the garments makes the wearer feel wet and uncomfortable when they take them off. Remember, getting cold and wet will make you vulnerable to hypothermia, even outside the winter months.

Always have a spare set of dry clothes. It is as important for morale as for safety. Keep them dry by using a rucksack liner – whatever they say, no rucksack is waterproof.

While we are on the subject of rucksacks, try not to economize too much purchasing one. Comfort is important and an ill-fitting or poorly designed one will cause fatigue very quickly. You probably will not go far wrong with adjustable back sacks made by Berghaus, Karrimor or Lowe. If you are camping, even with the lightest weight tents and sleeping bags, you will need at least a 55 litre rucksack to fit everything in – 65 is best. If you are staying in B&Bs you may get away with a 45 litre sack.

Try to keep the load in your rucksack down to 30lb (13.5kg) if you are camping and less if your hostelling or using bed and breakfast establishments.

If you are camping in the mountains make sure your tent is designed for that purpose. It is amazing how quickly weather can change at high altitudes and it's even more amazing how quickly it can demolish a 'low-level' tent. Ridge tents need A-poles for stability. More modern designs include geodesic dome tents with flexible poles and tunnel tents (not usually quite as stable in high winds). Check out those made by Wild Country, Phoenix and North Face.

Sleeping bags are rated in 'seasons'. A 1-2 season sleeping bag will suffice for late spring to early autumn. It would be uncomfortable if night-time temperatures came anywhere near 0°C. Conversely a heavy sleeping bag would be uncomfortably hot in even the English

summer. A 3-4 seasons bag is good enough for most English conditions though a 5 season (I wonder what the fifth season is?) would be needed for a Cairngorm winter. Synthetic fillings such as hollow fibre are bulkier than their down equivalents but offer more insulation when wet.

Make sure you are fully equipped with strong boots and ones which have been 'worn in'. Lightweight 3-4 season leather ones are probably best; fabric boots are usable if they have a waterproof membrane such as Goretex or Sympatex – without this they will leak like a sieve and you would end up with bad blisters and numb feet like wrinkled kippers. Do not go over the top with rigid 5-season mountain boots for a long-distance walk such as Lakeland to Lindisfarne. They will cause fatigue and also erode the footpaths more quickly. Finally, do not forget to pack some emergency medical supplies (plasters bandages *et cetera*). There are plenty of good kits around - see your local 'outdoor' shop.

Useful Reading

The Alternative Pennine Way – Denis Brook and Phil Hinchcliffe (Cicerone)
The Reivers Way – James Roberts (Cicerone)
The Pennine Mountains Terry Marsh (Hodder)
On Foot in the Pennines – Roly Smith (David & Charles)
The Northumbrian Coastline – Ian Smith (Sandhill Press)
In and Around Alnwick, Morpeth, Rothbury Warkworth – Ian Smith (Sandhill)
Discovering Northumberland – Ron and Marlene Freethy (John Donald)
A Portrait of Northumberland - Nancy Ridley (Hale)
Ordnance Survey Leisure Guide: Northumbria (OS/AA)
Ghosts and Legends of Northumbria – Coquet Editions
A Coast to Coast Walk – A. Wainwright (Michael Joseph)
England's Last Wilderness – David Bellamy and Brendan Quayle (Michael Joseph)
Walking the North Pennines - Paddy Dillon (Cicerone)
Pennine Ways – John Gillham (Crowood)
Britain's Highest Peaks – Jeremy Ashcroft (David & Charles)
100 Walks In Northumberland (Crowood)
Lakeland Mountains Vols 1 & 2 –Terry Marsh (Hodder)

I am also indebted to the various authors who produced an excellent series of walks leaflets for the East Cumbria Countryside Project.

Index